HOW TO WAT

John Arlott, writer and broadcaster, was born in
1914 at Basingstoke, Hampshire. Former cricket
correspondent of the *Guardian*, and President
of the Cricketers' Association since its foundation, he has been a policeman, BBC producer,
and a general instructor at the BBC Training
School. He has published a number of books of
poetry, and has written and broadcast on
cricket, wine – he is wine correspondent of the
Guardian – cheese, snuff, glass, aquatints,
Hampshire, and the Isles of Scilly. He stood as
Liberal candidate for Epping in the elections of
1955 and 1959.

John Arlott published *How to Watch Cricket* in 1948; and *How to Watch Cricket 1949* in the following year. This book employs the same title; but, as the text indicates, the game of cricket and, because of television, watching it, have changed so much in the interim that it has been completely rewritten.

In bringing the text up to date for this Fontana edition, the author has provided a fresh chapter on the counties.

HOW TO WATCH CRICKET

JOHN ARLOTT

Fontana/Collins

First published in Great Britain
by William Collins (Willow Books) 1983
First issued in Fontana Paperbacks,
revised and with a fresh chapter on the counties, 1984

Copyright © John Arlott 1983, 1984

Filmset in Monophoto Times
by Ace Filmsetting Ltd, Frome, Somerset
Reproduced, printed and bound in Great Britain by
Hazell Watson & Viney Limited,
Member of the BPCC Group,
Aylesbury, Bucks

In Memory,
S.W.H.
– Stan –
1902–1982
'and, mark you, a very fine bowler'

CONTENTS

ACKNOWLEDGMENTS

These are due primarily to Jack Bannister for passing his observant eye over the text – though he is not to blame for any of the book's errors. Thanks, too, are due to J. M. Brearley and Macdonald & Janes, publishers of *Wisden Cricketers' Almanack* 1982, for the quotation from Mr Brearley's 'Some Thoughts on Modern Captaincy'; to the executors of K. S. Ranjitsinhji and William Blackwood, the publishers, for an extract from *The Jubilee Book of Cricket*; to MCC for permission to quote from *The Laws of Cricket* (1982); to the TCCB for their definition of the Qualification and Registration Regulations; and to MCC and Heinemann for permission to reproduce diagrams of bowlers' grips from *The MCC Cricket Coaching Book*.

INTRODUCTION

The purpose of this book is to help the relatively inexperienced or semi-experienced spectator – whether at a match or through television – to derive more pleasure, or more pleasure sooner, than might otherwise be the case.

The point of watching cricket is pleasure. Many different people, though, derive different pleasures from the game. Some, indeed, seem to take pleasure in suffering; the partisan, overjoyed by his team winning, is likely to agonize over their defeat. Everyone who even remotely understands the game will respond to its drama. In fact a cricket match is fashioned rather like a play: the end is not always conclusive but, in compensation, at best it cannot be foreseen; and when its own dramatic unities – runs, wickets and time – fuse, they create the suspense of high drama. The technical observer will appreciate the skills or the style of the bowler or the style of the batsman; the strategy of the captain. The statistician – an increasing proportion and power in present-day following of the game – finds his pleasure in its figures, their analysis, and records. The general observer enjoys the grace and controlled effort; the wider and the pictorially minded, the play and counterplay of colour and movement in the pattern of white on green, linked to the motion of bat and ball; the more contemplative observer, the humanity of the players who, in the course of a six-and-a-half hour playing day, can scarcely conceal their true characters.

Most of those pleasures are distilled by the watcher himself – or, increasingly, herself – who requires little assistance. This brief study is designed to help towards the basic understanding which adds point to the play.

There is no point in watching cricket except for pleasure. Even the professional observer or reporter is wasting time – however much money he may earn – unless he finds enjoyment in it. To report the doings of parliament; the development of business or industry; the progress of a war, may be a grave and historic matter. Cricket, though, is a game; serious only in the extent of the pleasure it may give. Its reporting should be a record of pleasure.

That pleasure can be great; and the justification and reward of this book would be to heighten it.

Chapter 1

THE SIGNIFICANCE
OF FIRST-CLASS CRICKET

If chapter two will appear elementary to anyone who has played cricket at any level, the argument which follows is not always appreciated even by those of considerable experience at club level.

The first version of this book ought properly to have been called 'How to Watch First-class Cricket'; but that did not come happily off the tongue. Now the one-day cricket played by the counties is not classified as first-class, while to use simply the term 'county cricket' would be to exclude Test Matches. For the purpose of the immediate argument, however, first-class cricket may be taken to include one-day county matches.

The fact is that first-class cricket is an altogether more intense – or more professional (in the best sense of that word) – form of the game than that played by the majority of cricketers. A moment's thought will indicate that this is only to be expected when the counties perform for six to seven days a week for the best part of five months; with pre-season nets and practice and trial matches; while many of the players are engaged on tours, other overseas engagements, or coaching for most of the English winter.

Anyone with even short acquaintance with the first-class game has experienced this vast gap of difference. It is true that some club players have proved initially successful in county cricket. Only rarely, however, has anyone sustained the strain without a break. Perhaps the most important difference they experience is the far higher pace of first-class fast bowling. Certainly it is the margin first apparent to the newcomer. To have sat in the dressing room and watched this dawn upon a much respected top level club cricketer and good friend remains, even at nearly fifty years distance, a most salutary experience. It was his first county match: his two innings comprised two balls from Harold Larwood, three from Bill Voce, two edged singles and the stumps hit twice. He had centuries to his name in the club game; was a fit, nimble, quick-eyed young athlete; and he admitted he was lucky to get those two touches.

Even those who weather the initial, new-ball attack – and most

1

batsmen are blooded and grounded in the middle of the order – tend to find the strain of a long innings more than they can sustain until they have undergone a considerable hardening process.

Bowlers are always likely to enjoy greater initial success than batsmen. The batsman who makes an early impact is by no means always able to keep it up. Harold Gimblett, for instance, made the fastest hundred of the season in his first county match. Including that century, and in 14 more matches that season, he averaged only 17; and, as a recent biography shows, he subsequently suffered considerable mental anguish.

If bowlers more often make an initial impact, they tend to achieve it by novelty. A side whose batsmen have been troubled by a newcomer will soon be interrogated by other counties' players as to his particular qualities: all soon prepare their defences against him. So, while the young batsman may become hardened and do better in his second season than his first, the reverse is often true of bowlers who, once their novelty is 'rumbled', have to 'graft' for their subsequent wickets.

The simplest factor of the difference between the professional and the amateur game is physical. Any club cricketer knows the tiring effect of two or three hours in the field. A hot, six-hour day on a hard outfield; some twenty or so overs; or simply fielding – not merely the running but the constant alertness, moving in anticipation, towards every stroke played to every ball bowled – takes a considerable toll in fatigue. When Len Hutton first came into the Yorkshire side, although his batting talent was clear to see and he appeared in the opening fixture, he was so constantly rested that, despite an innings of 196, he was included in only 16 of their 35 matches; and such was the physical sapping effect of the first-class game – almost as much in the field as when batting – only 17 of 36 in the next year.

In the club game the batsman who lives through the early stages of his innings may expect to find the remainder of the bowling less taxing. At the higher level, there are few easy runs. The first-class batsman who reaches thirty or forty is expected to go on; the best of them often to make centuries. The newcomer, though, is always likely to be tired by the concentration demanded. The difference between the middle of the bat and the edge is, after all, only two inches; a pitiful margin of error over a two-, three- or four-hour innings. Add the skilful probing of a batsman's technique and the ruthless exploitation of his weaknesses; the high standard of field-placing and catching, and the professional intensity of the first-class game is apparent. At Test level the pressure is even greater.

That is the setting for all that follows here. The television and radio commentators invariably describe what is going on, and indicate its significance. Some, however, are simply not familiar with the terms they use. The following chapter attempts to provide basic background information. The glossary at the end will explain technical terms, the laws, and the relevant notes on them.

Diagram of Cricket Pitch

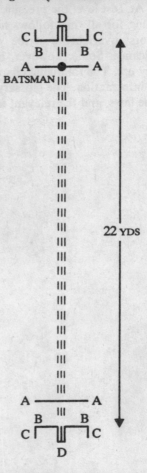

Here is a diagram of the pitch. The traditional measurements have been scrupulously retained, hence the metric equivalents may not seem particularly easy to memorize. The broken lines emphasize the line of wicket to wicket.

   Length 22 yards/20.12m from wicket to wicket.

A *Popping crease* 4 feet/1.22m from stumps: deemed 'unlimited in length'.

B *Bowling crease* 8 feet 8 inches/2.64m long with the stumps in the middle.

C *Return crease* to mark outer limits of bowling crease: deemed 'unlimited in length'.

D *Wicket* 9 inches/22.86cm wide, 28 inches/71.1cm high, bails each $4\frac{3}{8}$ inches/11.1cm long.

Chapter 2

SETTING THE SCENE

(for beginner watchers)

For the sake of clarity it would be best to establish the simpler definitions at once. To anyone who has played cricket this will be almost painfully elementary. For many, however, watching the game for the first time on television or during a day out – probably a benefit match on some country ground – it is crucially important if they are to understand the action and any kind of comment.

Although, at the highest level of performance, cricket is probably the most profound game in the world, it is in essence simple. Played between two sides of eleven players and controlled by two umpires – one at each end of the pitch and who are 'the sole judges of fair and unfair play' – it has been described as 'casting a ball at three straight sticks and defending the same with a fourth'.

The ball, which may be made of plastic or composition but is usually of leather stitched round a cork-wrapped core, must weigh not less than $5\frac{1}{2}$ nor more than $5\frac{3}{4}$ ounces; and its circumference must be between $8\frac{13}{16}$ and 9 inches. The 'three straight sticks' – in fact three at each end of the pitch – are stumps; arranged side by side, close enough to prevent the ball passing between them, in a group 28 inches high and 9 inches wide, with two bails, each $4\frac{3}{8}$ inches long, resting in grooves at the top.

The bowler may bowl right arm or left, underarm, round-arm or over-arm, and from whichever side of the wicket he chooses; though he must communicate his choice to the umpire, who will tell the batsman what it is.

The bowler must bowl – not throw – the ball: with his 'back' foot within and not touching the return crease; and with some part of his 'front' foot, whether grounded or raised, behind the popping crease. He bowls in 'overs' of six (by special arrangement eight) balls each. An unfair delivery – 'no-ball' – or a wide is not counted in the over.

The fourth 'straight stick' is the bat: a sprung handle spliced into a wooden blade. whose overall length may not be more than 38 inches; and whose width may not be more than $4\frac{1}{4}$ inches.

The batsman scores by hitting the ball and, if he and his partner

Plan of field showing the fielding positions in general use

Here is a plan of the most general fielding positions. They assume, as does the text, unless the contrary is stated, that the batsman is right-handed; and that the bowler is delivering right-arm over the wicket.

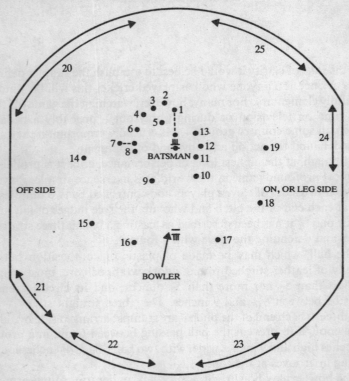

CLOSE CATCHERS
1. Wicketkeeper
2. First slip
3. Second slip
4. Third slip
5. Short slip
6. Gully
7. Backward point
8. Point
9. Silly mid-off
10. Silly mid-on
11. Forward short leg
12. Short leg
13. Backward short leg

MIDFIELD
14. Cover point
15. Extra cover
16. Mid-off
17. Mid-on
18. Mid-wicket
19. Square leg

OUTFIELD
20. Third man
21. Deep extra cover
22. Long-off
23. Long-on
24. Deep square leg
25. Long leg

can cross and make good their ground at the opposite crease, that counts as one run. They may run and cross as often as they wish so long as the fielding side do not break the wicket of a batsman out of his ground. He scores four runs if the struck ball crosses the boundary line after touching the ground; six if it crosses over, and clear of, the boundary line.

A batsman may be out in the following ten ways:

(1) *Bowled* when the bowled ball breaks the wicket – i.e. causes a bail to fall – even though the ball has touched the batsman's bat or body or clothing. (Law 30)

(2) *Timed Out* if he wilfully takes more than two minutes after the fall of the previous wicket to come to the crease. This is rarely invoked; the key word is 'wilfully' and the law was framed to prevent deliberate time-wasting. (Law 31)

(3) *Caught* when the ball touches the bat – or the batsman's hand or glove holding the bat below the wrist – and is held by a fieldsman before it touches the ground. (Law 32)

(4) *Handled the Ball* if he touches the ball with a hand not holding the bat; unless he does so with the consent of the fielding side. (Law 33)

(5) *Hit Ball Twice* if, after he has played the ball, or stopped it with his body, he strikes it again except for the purpose of protecting his wicket. (Law 34)

(6) *Hit Wicket* if he breaks the wicket with any part of his bat, person, or equipment, in the course of playing a stroke or setting off for his first run. (Law 35)

(7) *Obstructing the Field* if he wilfully obstructs the opposite side by word or action. (Law 37)

(8) *Run Out* if, when he is out of his ground, the wicket is put down by a member of the opposite side. If the batsmen have crossed, the one running to the wicket that is put down is out; if they have not crossed, the one running from it is out. (Note, though, this does not include being stumped: *see* 9). (Law 38)

(9) *Stumped* when, having received a ball, he is out of his ground and the wicketkeeper, without any other fieldsman being involved, puts down the wicket. Except, of course, if he is attempting a run, when he would be run out. (Law 39)

(10) *Leg Before Wicket (LBW)*   when, with any part of his body or equipment except his bat, he intercepts a ball which, in the opinion of the umpire, would have hit the wicket: provided that (a) the ball pitched in a straight line between wicket and wicket; or (b) the ball pitched on the off-side of the striker's wicket; *and* (c) the point of interception is in a straight line between wicket and wicket

or (d) the point of interception is outside the line of the off stump *but* the batsman made no attempt to play the ball. (Law 36)

The proviso (d) was introduced to prevent deliberate pad-play. This is probably the most contentious Law – or, at least, it produces the most contentious umpiring decisions. Therefore it is worth including these drawings (*see* opposite) showing how difficult it can be to assess an lbw decision (as W. G. Grace once demonstrated to a group of players – and umpires – with a length of cotton); and why certain decisions are given (*see* page 10).

W. G. Grace's Experiment

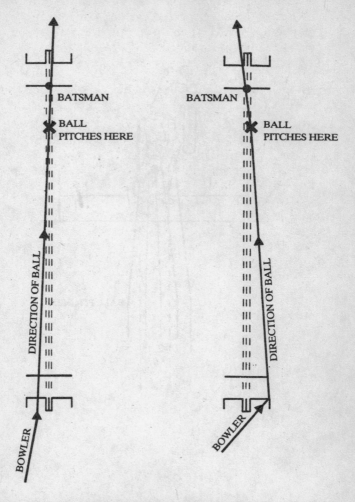

An adaptation of W. G. Grace's method of demonstrating the immense difficulty of making certain lbw decisions. The diagrams, drawn to scale, show how:

Left A straight ball delivered from a point only 18 inches from the stumps and pitching on a fair-length spot (8 feet in front of the batsman) and on the middle stump will miss the leg stump.

Right A straight ball delivered right-arm round the wicket and pitching on a fair-length spot on the leg stump will miss the off stump.

The LBW Rule

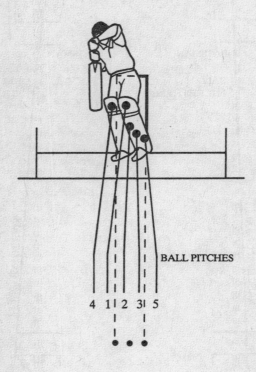

BALL PITCHES

1 **OUT**   The ball pitched outside the off stump but hit the pad on the line of the stumps and would have hit the wicket.

2 **OUT**   Pitched on and would have hit.

3 **OUT**   Pitched leg, moved towards off but would still have hit the stumps.

4 **OUT/NOT OUT**   Ball pitched outside the line and hit the pad, also outside the line; but would have hit the wicket. **NOT OUT** if the striker made a genuine attempt to play the ball; **OUT** if he did not.

5 **NOT OUT**   The ball pitched outside the line of the leg stump.

Chapter 3

THE CHANGING FACE
OF CRICKET

The first version of this book was being written in 1947. At that time, the watching of cricket seemed to its raw author a clear matter: not without profundity, certainly, but straightforward. In the subsequent quarter of a century that opinion has altered. So, too, has cricket, and watching it, though the game has not, perhaps, changed so violently as some of the older generation argue. Indeed, it may well be that watching, or at least the attitude to watching, has changed more than the game itself.

To examine the clear changes: it could be said in 1947 that the book should more properly be called 'Watching First-class Cricket'; and that 'first-class' meant the play of the counties, the Test-playing touring sides, the three-day fixtures of MCC, and of Oxford and Cambridge Universities. Now an important proportion of the spectrum consists of the one-day competitions which are not – for the moment at least – defined as first-class. On the other hand, the Universities can now only by courtesy be described as first-class. In 1947, Oxford and Cambridge between them included Martin Donnelly (one of the finest of modern left-handed batsmen), Doug Insole, Abdul Hafeez Kardar, Trevor Bailey, P. A. Whitcombe (hailed, briefly but not without justification, as an English fast-bowling hope), Guy Willatt, Ron Maudsley and Tony Mallett. The year of its publication saw the appearances of John Dewes, Hubert Doggart, Clive van Ryneveld, Donald Carr and 'Buck' Divecha. Nine of them became Test players, a tenth played in wartime representative matches, and a number of others won, and well deserved, county places.

Many present-day spectators were watching cricket as long ago as 1947. It may be well to examine the changes which have taken place in the interim, and their extent. The value of such an assessment may be to clarify what tends to be an emotional response. Most followers of cricket are, at heart, romantic about it; at best subjective. Some perceive little change over the past quarter century; others believe – and decry the fact – that it has changed too much and

11

too violently. Cricket would not be true to tradition in reflecting the society in which it is played if the phases of social change were not apparent in it. The truth probably is that it has developed – and that probably is the right word – considerably: that the changes have not been fundamental but rather a matter of degree. Indeed, it may be argued that the game itself has altered less than the watching of it, which has been completely transformed by television.

The whole British social fabric has changed radically since 1947. Throughout, the major influence for change has undoubtedly been financial. Cricket has been no exception. Until the Second World War, county cricket barely gave a thought to its solvency. It was sustained by gate money, membership subscriptions and, at the pinch, by aristocratic patronage. Since then, apart from the gloriously euphoric upsurge of support in the immediate post-war years – the re-start; the 1947 summer of Denis Compton and Bill Edrich; the tour of Bradman's 1948 Australians – attendances have fallen. Because the game's administrators could not imagine the possibility of insolvency, they did not increase subscriptions to keep pace with expenditure; and, crucially, the wealthy patrons of old had been taxed out of the position to hold the balance, while the supporters' clubs which temporarily replaced them could not hold the balance.

The former captive audiences gradually disappeared, wooed away by the pleasures of increased incomes, and leisure time, and widely extended car ownership. The harsh economic realities of the situation were brought home. The major attempt to lure them back or, as some would argue, to create a fresh extra public, consisted of one-day, over-limit matches; first in 1963 through the Gillette Cup (since 1981 called the NatWest Bank Trophy); then in 1964 through the most revolutionary Sunday play of the John Player League; and, finally, in 1972, through the Benson & Hedges Cup, on a league/knock-out basis.

The economic aspect of cricket is more significant and more far-reaching than many of its followers realize. Although it was not, by wider standards, a well-paid profession, it tended, until the abolition of the maximum wage in Association Football in 1961, generally to attract, on financial grounds, the athletic young men who often in England have aptitudes for both cricket and football. At least it was, too, until recently, possible for a man to play both games at professional level: that is no longer so.

Above all, the economic difference between the two games is so wide that cricket is at an almost ludicrous disadvantage in competing for talented youngsters. During 1982, the TCCB, on behalf of the counties, agreed to a minimum wage of £6750 for capped professionals, with scaled-down figures for the uncapped. Certainly, too, some counties pay over the minimum while a dozen or so outstanding representative players might make double that, or rather more; and two or three, with side-earnings from public appearances, sponsorship and advertising, may receive a dozen times as much. On the other hand, several dozen British Association footballers make over £60,000 from their clubs alone; one, probably, in the region of £100,000. Many of them also receive considerable on-the-side incomes. Moreover, while cricket is an extremely precarious living (ten years is a more than average career) and limited to some 180 capped players, there are some 2000 Football League soccer professionals in Britain; and probably another 500 taking something more than pin-money from clubs in the lesser leagues. Cricket simply does not compare with football in terms of income or security.

Now, therefore, the financial situation, and the pattern of football fixtures, combine to make it probable that, if Jack Hobbs, Wally Hammond, Patsy Hendren, Denis Compton, Bill Edrich, Brian Close, Arthur Milton, Fred Trueman and Willy Watson were all now seventeen years old, their parents, school masters, or career guidance officers would be hard put indeed to advise them to take up professional cricket in preference to football.

Socially, too, in the interim between the editions of this book, the official status of the amateur cricketer has disappeared. That, though, largely represented the removal of an anomaly.

The more obvious changes in play have been created chiefly by the presence of over-limit cricket. This form of the game had, of course, existed for years at club level, where the same merit as now commended it to county treasurers – quick entertainment and a result in hours instead of days. A minority – a substantial and informed one, but a minority nevertheless – argued, from the time the one-day county competitions were first mooted, that they would damage the quality of high-level performance.

The fundamental weakness of the over-limit game in terms of its relationship to the three-day and five-day games is its inherent negation of one of the essential factors of the full game. Traditionally, the game of cricket revolves round runs, wickets and time. Over-limit play is not concerned with wickets. In terms of success there, a team does better to restrict its opponents to 150 for no wicket than to bowl them out for 151.

Any captain faced with that problem is virtually bound to do what county captains have done: employ defensive bowling methods to restrictive fields, placed to save runs rather than make catches. Most have tended, too – although the figures do not entirely confirm their methods – to rely on even mediocre medium-pace bowling in preference to spin; while the spinners they do use tend to push the ball through flat.

Batsmen, for their part, have had to accept a fresh dichotomy. To illustrate it at its most extreme, a county batsman opening his team's innings in a Championship match an hour or so from the end of play on a Saturday and, because others are out, needing to build a safe innings, moves on to a John Player League match on the Sunday. There he is required to improvise, slog, take risks for quick runs. On Monday he returns to his three-day innings. There were those who prophesied that, as a result of the conflicting demands of the two forms of the game, batsmen would become less sound; less capable of building an innings; and that performance at Test level would deteriorate. English Test batting has, in fact, declined but it is not proven that this is a result of over-limit cricket as distinct from a diminution in the supply of talent. It was said, too, that spin bowlers, in particular, would tend to lose their attacking edge. The decline in both the amount and the quality of spin bowling in the first-class game supports that argument.

On the other hand, it is beyond all question that over-limit cricket has improved the standard of fielding. There were signs of development along those lines in the cricket of the late 1940s and 1950s with increasing study of field-placing. That led to the emergence of such specialist close fieldsmen, most of them at short-leg, as Allan Watkins, Tony Lock, Wilfred Wooller, Stuart Surridge and Jack Ikin, who virtually ruled out the leg-glance as a 'business' stroke. It was, though, the high-pressure one-day fielding – primarily of Lancashire under Jack Bond – which lifted that department to heights it had never reached before.

That, in its turn, demanded such a high standard of fitness and speed in the field as the masters of old – like Hobbs, Rhodes, Woolley, Mead and Sutcliffe – who continued playing into their fifties, could never have mustered under such pressure.

It would, though, be a mistake to attribute all the developments to the over-limit game. True to its cue, and reflecting its social background, cricket in the late fifties and early sixties passed through a phase best described as technological. It would be an exaggeration to attribute this entirely to M. J. K. Smith but for many observers he personified it. An innovator in rugby football also – his half-back combination with Onllwyn Brace opened up fresh vistas in that game – he applied a shrewd mind to cricket. He was concerned with effect rather than romance; and, although he could stroke the ball through the covers as handsomely as anyone, he considered that to be un-economic against the normal packed off-side field-setting for slow left-arm spin. He believed that type of bowling to be vulnerable. Although there were many to disagree with him and argue that it must be played to the off-side, he demonstrated that the orthodox slow left-arm finger-spinner could be hit profitably through the leg-side. The initial justification of the theory demanded a player of Mike Smith's high ability. Once, though, he had achieved it, others followed him in destroying the entire field-placing and overall strategy of traditional slow left-arm spin. Soon, too, related methods were applied to the right-arm off-spinner. Similar pragmatism had for some time been applied to wrist-spin. Instead of attacking it in the old-fashioned way, batsmen defended against the good length ball and waited to punish the loose one. Few wrist-spinners both turned the ball enough and kept a sufficiently accurate length and line to compel respectful treatment six balls to the over. As a result, the wrist-spinner has been all but eliminated from the English game.

That is not to argue that wrist-spin is no longer important. Its significance has been emphasized for many years since it suffered neglect in England. England – with apologies to Robin Hobbs – barely employed a genuine leg-spinner at Test level after Roly Jenkins (1948–52). Doug Wright was a phenomenon, a medium-paced leg-spinner, whose main technical significance lay in his googly; while the immensely likeable Eric Hollies was a 'roller' rather than a true spinner: accurate, but not the man to produce the fiery unplayable ball.

Since the Second World War, Australia have savaged England with such wrist-spinners as McCool, Dooland, Iverson – of the freakish spin-method – Benaud, Gleeson, Jenner and O'Keeffe. Ramadhin and the Indian Chandrasekhar have also harried English batsmen. Most lately, the Pakistani Abdul Qadir – whose figures did him less than justice – puzzled all the English batsmen of 1982 and, with just reward, those of Australia in the following months.

It has been argued that the English climate is antipathetic to wrist-spin; that it chills the fingers too often for wrist-spin to flourish; and that it produces pitches unhelpful to their type of turn. Still, even though it is being allowed – tragically – to die out in the English county game, it should never pass out of the mind of the English watcher. Not only may visiting teams employ it valuably in Tests but, at any time, such a practitioner as Bruce Dooland, George Tribe, Jack Walsh, Colin McCool or Abdul Qadir may appear to wreak similar damage among English batsmen unaccustomed to it in the normal traffic of the county game.

Meanwhile the finger-spinners have virtually abandoned flight, preferring safely to 'push it through' defensively flat and, by comparison with their classic forebears, short of the length they maintained by the ability to deceive batsmen 'through the air'.

The history of cricket, however, is of batsmen and bowlers planning to counter one another's tactics and advantages. If the power of the spinner waned, that of the 'seam' bowler – usually by tightly controlled inswing to a safe-catching group of close leg-side fieldsmen – increased. For a period they held the game or, at least, that of all but the best batsmen, in a savage grip. Gradually, though, batsmen contrived to 'work' – significant word – them through the leg-side field, eschewing the established and long profitable leg-glance because it lifted the ball off the ground by the few inches which were enough for the prehensile backward short-leg to scoop up the catch. Instead, they deflected, pushed the full length ball, while pressing the bowler to drop short and proffer the opportunity to sweep or hook.

The next move came from the bowlers. Intimidatory fast bowling has been employed as a legitimate tactic since cricket began. Through the seventies it became more and more established idiom. Historically the great fast bowlers had hunted in pairs; probably because it was rare for a country to have more than two – though England might have mustered four about 1954-5-6. That meant that the batsman who held on through the double-harness attack might expect to come through to calmer and more productive waters. Lately, though, West Indies have found themselves with four – more at a pinch – and, realistically enough, they have employed them in an all but unbroken battery of high pace. Legislation has been introduced to limit, but not to outlaw, the use of the 'bouncer'. It is still – as it always must be – permitted and, even if it is restricted to one an over, the mounting skill of bowlers in threatening or concealing it makes it a considerable weapon even, paradoxically, when it is not actually delivered. By bowling it from the edge of the crease so that the ball 'follows' the batsman, bowlers ultimately made it such a deadly weapon that batsmen were driven to the protection of the helmet: visually the greatest change in post-1945 cricket. There, for the moment, rests the unending batsman–bowler competition, in which each constantly studies and spars for advantage.

It is arguable that, over the past quarter-century, the watching of cricket has changed more than the game itself. When Test cricket restarted in England in 1946, the BBC – then our sole television service – broadcast only Tests from London (Lord's and The Oval); extending to Nottingham in 1950; Leeds and Old Trafford in 1952; Edgbaston in 1957. Thus the availability of television broadcasting of Test Matches is still only twenty-five years old. Moreover, there was by no means widespread ownership of television until relatively late in the period. So the emphasis in spectatorship was, for some time, on personal attendance. Much more of it now is through television or, for people driving cars or otherwise unable to watch television, by listening to sound radio. By far the largest audience for Test Matches and other selected fixtures is now through television.

In yet another attempt to increase revenue, it was decided in 1968 to allow each county to introduce one overseas player for three years by Special Registration. In a series of changes in the relevant legislation that number was later increased to two. The number has recently been reduced on grounds that these introductions have hindered the development of home talent. That is open to question; but certainly, in its early days, the scheme admitted players such as Garfield Sobers, Barry Richards, Rohan Kanhai, Mike Procter, Asif Iqbal, who added considerably to the attractions of the domestic game and served as admirable models for young English cricketers; while Farokh Engineer and Clive Lloyd gave an immense fillip to Lancashire cricket through successes in the one-day game.

A major and, as it may yet emerge, one of the most far-reaching changes on the playing side of cricket in the last twenty-five years, was created by the administrators. While the Laws of Cricket still state 'The pitch shall not be completely covered during a match unless prior arrangement or regulations so provide', match regulations now stipulate that it may be covered for the night before the match begins; on every night of the match, and as soon as rain stops play. Thus one of the historic elements of English cricket – the sticky wicket – or even the slow, wet-turner, is, presumably, obviated for ever. It means, too, that the demise of the finger-spinner – the right-arm off-break, or left-arm breakaway bowler – is hastened. Some of the epic performances of English cricket history – the killer spin bowling or the high batting skills against the turning ball – are ruled out for the future. Perhaps the decision, in so far as it affects Test Matches, was justified in the interests of fairness to visiting countries; but, for the domestic game, one of its most dramatic features has been removed. This must mean that, because of the defensive value of their accuracy, the fast-medium and medium-pace 'seam-up' bowlers will tend more and more to take over from the spinners.

Off the field the most significant development has been the extension of television coverage. Now, every ball of every Test Match of a home series can be watched on BBC television. This also makes an important contribution to the finances of the game; though not so great as it would do if commercial television competed for the rights as it does in Australia. Here, presumably, the commercial companies do not consider cricket sufficiently attractive to the sections of their audience most sensitive to advertising.

The television watcher now has the most perfect cricket spectator service that has ever existed. Of old, the enthusiasts at a match used to strive to position themselves behind the bowler's arm. There was, though, only room for a few people there; and even they often could not position themselves high enough to see, as it were, over the shoulder of the umpire and the bowler; and, obviously, none could be behind the bowler's arm at both ends. The present-day television spectator, though, is given precisely that service; plus a close-up – through 'zoom' – better even than field glasses could afford; views, too, not only of batsman and bowler but, through other cameras, of fieldsmen as well. Moreover, embarrassing as it may be, especially for umpires but also, sometimes, for players, there is the facility of the playback, in true, or slow, motion, or both: which no in-the-flesh spectator can ever have had, but which is now an automatic part of television presentation. As if to make complete nonsense of the argument for 'atmosphere', 'reality' and 'actually being there', the viewer is granted also Test Match players, experts and captains, to describe the course of play and to comment on its progress, strategy and quality of performance. To complete all – as anyone who has fought for food and drink on some of the seedier Test grounds will appreciate – the television viewer can choose, control and time his – or her – own food, drink, physical comfort – and sleep away stoppages for rain.

Chapter 4

THE WICKET

Every cricket match is conditioned, and shaped, by the pitch, generally called – perversely as it must seem to the uninitiated – the wicket (which is also the term used for the groups of three stumps at each end). Most pitches prepared for first-class matches are – or the groundsman who prepares them intends them to be – good. That means good for batting; that the ball will not deviate unaccountably (often not at all) and will come through at an even pace and height, neither too fast nor too slow for the making of controlled strokes.

Various mischances may frustrate the groundsman. A long spell of rain may prevent him from using a heavy roller to produce a true surface; a long drought may compel heavy watering, which does not have the same 'natural' effect as rain – and which may result in a really wet pitch if there is heavy rain immediately before the match.

In general there are six types of wicket:

(1) The *good* (plumb, true or easy) wicket, where batsmen will expect to make runs because neither seam nor spin bowlers will be able to make the ball deviate appreciably, nor surprisingly.

(2) The *green* or *green topped* wicket, which is likely to be the most frequent variant from 'good' in these days of covered pitches, because it is created generally by a moist atmosphere – which covers cannot shut out – rather than by rain. The green wicket is invariably well grassed; and it is identifiable because the ball leaves a dark mark where it pitches. Its effect is to allow medium to fast 'seam' bowling, in which the seam is held more or less vertically and delivered with a swing-bowler's action to angle or 'move' after pitching; sometimes in contradiction to the direction of the swing. Since this effect is not compellable by the bowler nor, therefore, foreseeable by the batsman, it poses considerable problems.

3) The *fair* wicket, of which Bradford was formerly the classic example (and Tunbridge Wells and Southend, now, probably are the best), allows both seam and spin bowlers to achieve some degree of movement, but at even pace and even height. It is the ideal – in dressing-room parlance 'a good cricket wicket' – but, alas, nowadays, all too rare.

(4) The *sporting* wicket, possibly deteriorating to *fiery*, generally results from a period of drought; dry, hard soil under grass. Fast bowling can be lethal in such conditions.

(5) The *crumbling* pitch also results from dry weather and usually, also, lack of grass to bind it up. Spinners and, even more, medium-pace 'cutters', profit from such conditions.

(6) The *rough* pitch should not occur; but it does, usually through misjudgement on the part of the groundsman. It does not give batsmen a fair chance. The ball does not come off it truly.

The additional, and important, further factor in the conditions which is not dictated by the pitch is that of atmosphere. The mechanics of swing bowling are not fully understood. It is, though, certain that in some climatic conditions a cricket ball, because of the unevenness created by the seam, will deviate from straight through the air. That happened, and was recorded, in the eighteenth century days of Hambledon, when bowling was all underarm, and it has persisted ever since. No one is quite certain of the requisite conditions; but humidity probably is the major influence. The whole matter is made the more baffling by the fact that sometimes when a worn ball has swung violently, an apparently identical new ball from the same maker which, in theory, because of its more shiny surface would normally be expected to swing more, simply goes straight on.

Related to swing because it is produced by swing-bowling actions, movement off the seam on a 'green' wicket is assumed to result from the ball pitching on the seam at a slight angle to the ground. This, too, is something of a mystery; but that it happens is beyond all possible doubt.

Presumably we shall never again – except in the improbable event of a heavy storm falling before the covers can be put on the wicket – see a wet or 'sticky' wicket, for which batsmen will be grateful and which spin bowlers, the poor relations of the modern game, will resent. In Australia there will, of course, be what they may call a 'sticky wicket' because it happens generally after a cloudburst of such proportions that the water floods under the covers. Whereas an English 'sticky' was exploited by slow spin bowlers who made the ball turn sharply and quickly, an Australian 'sticky' is used by the faster bowlers who make the ball rise steeply and dangerously as happened in the Brisbane Tests of 1936, 1946 and 1950, and those at Sydney and Melbourne in 1936.

The spectator cannot always estimate at once the exact character of a pitch, but he can observe its pace; though that must be qualified by the effect of the roller. Before the start of play on each day of a match, and also between innings, seven minutes are allotted to sweeping and rolling the pitch. If the batting captain – who makes the decision – calls for the heavy roller, that generally indicates that he wants the pitch 'toned' or bound up. If he asks for the light one it may be assumed that he thinks the pitch so good (for batting) that it requires only cosmetic treatment. The exception occurs when, perhaps, he only has a few tail-end wickets to fall and does not want to tone down the wicket by the use of a heavy roller but keep it lively for his opponents' innings. Though, again, in similar circumstances he may call for a heavy in the hope that it will break up a pitch with a tendency to crumble so that the ball may move disconcertingly during the other side's innings. A captain whose side has the best part of an innings to bat will generally ask for a heavy roller to 'tame' the pitch, though, after rain, it can force moisture to the surface.

The pace of the pitch is indicated by the setting of the field. If it is fast, mid-on, mid-off and cover-point will be set straighter than usual; if slow, they will be more square. Batsmen vary in their predilection for forward or back play, but generally on a fast wicket they will play forward hoping to smother any movement; on a slow one, they have time to go back and estimate the movement of the ball before committing themselves to a stroke.

The opinion of the captain who wins the toss may be – roughly – gauged by his decision whether to bat or invite his opponents to do so. An old cricketing adage, though, says 'When you win the toss, always think of putting the other side in; but then bat.' In the over-limit game – invariably played on bland, covered wickets – the decision to bat or bowl often seems more a matter of superstition than calculation. On the other hand, the captains of strong batting sides may fancy their chances to chase a total; others, whose strength lies in bowling, like to put themselves in the position of not needing too many runs.

In the present time of covered pitches, captains usually ask their opponents to bat on pitches with a reputation – usually as a result of the method of preparation – for being 'green' in the early stages and subsequently drying out. When, as at Lord's, a wicket is known to wear, and to grant turn late in a three-day match, the captain winning the toss will invariably bat; as, indeed, most will do on the – now rapidly decreasing – 'casual' county wickets prepared by part-time and inexperienced groundsmen.

There follows a list of the main grounds on which county cricket is played and their normal characteristics. They may be altered by groundsmen (sometimes, it has been alleged, in order to suit and help the county's particular bowling strength); and must, of course, vary with the weather (though, since the introduction of covering, less than formerly). In the case of county headquarters, standards can generally be relied upon. In recent years the matter has often been different in the case of occasional, club or, more especially, local authority, grounds, where present restrictions on, and high cost of, labour often result in less, and less experienced, staffing and, hence, less thoroughness of, and consistency in, preparation.

DERBYSHIRE

Derby slow, and, as a rule, with sadly little life.
Chesterfield traditionally a lively, green, seamers' pitch.

ESSEX

Chelmsford generally low and slow, but varies according to how much grass is left on.
Ilford formerly fast and true; latterly has granted turn.
Southend an excellent cricket wicket; with some pace and turn, it gives all types of bowlers the chance to exert their skills; but is true for the good batsman.
Colchester a fair batting wicket but sometimes (according to the amount of grass) helpful to seam bowling; uneven in 1983.

GLAMORGAN

Cardiff inclines to be low and slow; safe for batsmen but little help to stroke-makers.
Swansea once a sandy turner; has lately become more sound and true. Groundsman Clements was runner-up for the award in 1982.

GLOUCESTERSHIRE

Bristol extremely low and slow; granting some turn but comfortable for batting, especially off the front foot; since 1982 occasionally uneven in bounce, with some help for seam bowlers.

Gloucester generally a good batting wicket; but occasionally helpful to spin.

Cheltenham a bowler's pitch; invariably turns at some point; and often seams in damp conditions.

HAMPSHIRE

Southampton a good batting pitch.

Bournemouth little pace; usually turns; unreliable since 1982.

Portsmouth not so lively as formerly but usually helps seam bowlers.

Basingstoke easy paced; usually a good batting wicket; short boundaries.

KENT

Reported uniformly the best in 1983.

Canterbury slow and easy; pleasant ground for spectators.

Dartford usually helps spinners.

Tunbridge Wells a good cricket wicket with something for the good bowler and the good batsman.

Maidstone usually green and helpful to seam bowling.

Folkestone much improved; sometimes helpful to spin.

LANCASHIRE

Manchester basically good for batting but variable according to the weather; can rapidly become helpful to seam or spin.

Liverpool slow, inclined to be spongy.

Southport a fine fast batting wicket.

Blackpool slow, but often with help for bowlers of most types.

LEICESTERSHIRE

Leicester generally flat, but much depends on how much grass is left.

Hinckley generally an honest club wicket; tends to be slow and comfortable for batting.

MIDDLESEX

Jim Fairbrother of Lord's won the Groundsman of the Year award in 1982: a remarkable achievement considering the immense weight of traffic the pitch carries.

Lord's on the slow and easy side; always likely to turn on the third day.

Uxbridge has generally produced interesting cricket; not so fast, nor so hard, as it was.

NORTHAMPTONSHIRE

Northampton slow; desperately hard work for bowlers.
Wellingborough usually helpful to spin; variable.

NOTTINGHAMSHIRE

Trent Bridge traditionally the classic true fast pitch for fast bowlers and stroke-making batsmen. Latterly it has given bowlers more help than formerly; and at times in 1981 was described as dangerous: subsequently reported.

SOMERSET

Taunton usually slow and easy-paced; though sometimes the ball will swing sharply and late within its high fencing.

Bath the low-lying riverside pitch has a chequered history; generally it helps bowlers of all types, but especially those using the seam, more than batsmen. Usually produces a positive result.

Weston-super-Mare not a reliable pitch; although it lacks hardness, the ball will sometimes fly. Another 'results' ground; given three days of play it invariably yielded a positive outcome. Banned after 1982.

SURREY

The Oval lately became so deadly slow and easy that it was decided to re-lay the square; but the new pitches have not lived up to their early promise, and are often uneven in bounce.

Guildford initially true; inclined to wear. .

SUSSEX

Hove potentially the most interesting pitch in the country; sea air can produce swing; or 'fret' which induces seam movement; but it has truth and pace for batsmen. As with so many present-day wickets, much depends on how much grass the groundsman leaves. *Eastbourne* it used to be, in batsmen's terms, 'a beauty': but banned after 1982.

WARWICKSHIRE

Edgbaston generally one of the most easy-paced wickets in the country; but, under cloud-cover, the ball will often swing alarmingly. *Nuneaton* once taken off the list for unsatisfactory surfaces; but now back in service and much better, generally true, granting some help to seam bowling.
Coventry slow and spongy, hampering stroke-play; the lateral boundaries, though, are shorter than any others in the country, which can result in freak scores.

WORCESTERSHIRE

Worcester was easy-paced; now often uneven in bounce, yet all too few positive results are achieved.
Stourbridge a good Birmingham League club wicket; true but tends to wear on the third day.

YORKSHIRE

Headingley variable; in good weather an easy batting pitch; under cloud, or in damp conditions, helps seam bowling; too often the bounce can be irregular; rarely helps spin.
Bradford nowadays flatter and with less life than of old.
Sheffield fair but often seams alarmingly in damp conditions.
Harrogate good batting wicket.
Scarborough usually a good batting wicket of fair pace.
Middlesbrough a good natural wicket, where the ball will move off the seam.

CAMBRIDGE UNIVERSITY

Fenner's not the immaculate batting wicket it was; often uneven: but, at its best, fast.

OXFORD UNIVERSITY

The Parks like Fenner's it is used for first-class cricket only at the start of the season when the weather is often unfavourable. Generally fast, conducive to stroke-play, but, in spring weather, often helps bowlers.

It is a matter for some regret that the earnest exhortations of authority to counties and groundsmen to prepare fast, true wickets have been virtually ignored. There are fewer such pitches now even than there were immediately after the war, when many had long been ill-tended. This must be one of the contributory factors in the decline of wrist-spin. There are far more wickets of uneven bounce than there were. This must in consequence deprive batsmen of full confidence and persuade some bowlers to rely on the irregularities of the pitch.

Several grounds have been banned in the past but the decision is not irrevocable and they are usually reinstated if and when good pitches are produced.

Chapter 5

GOING TO THE MATCH

For the in-the-flesh spectator, English first-class matches fall into two completely different categories. On the one hand, the three-day matches of the Schweppes County Championship and run-of-the-mill one-day games; on the other, Test Matches and the important one-day fixtures of the more successful sides.

Championship matches – alas for the county exchequers – are never nowadays crowded; neither are the one-day games not ultimately significant. Test Matches are widely recognized as 'occasions'; and attract many not genuinely interested in cricket. Key over-limit games draw both genuine county followers and, especially on Sundays, a froth of soccer-type 'supporters'.

In any event, the most comfortable way to watch any first-class match is as a member from the pavilion. The subscription to the county clubs which do not house Tests is very cheap: for those where Tests are played it is quite reasonable by comparison with normal prices of admission for the public. Problems lie in the fact that members cannot introduce their friends, wives – or even their mistresses – to the pavilion at Tests.

Nevertheless, at any match, important or minor, the greatest convenience and comfort is available to members, who have room to sit in comparative comfort (compared, that is, with normal public facilities) and can generally buy better refreshments.

At a three-day Championship match, comfort and convenience may be assumed. The catering may not be of *haute cuisine* standard, but it will be adequate, because it is normal and the caterers are accustomed to it – though even they must take precautions against days rained off and the consequent wasted provender.

Test Matches are a caterer's horror. If the weather is fine, or even if play is suspended, they may feed 30,000 people. If there is steady rain from morning, hardly anyone will come: they are left with an army of cooks, waitresses, barmen and porters and a mountain of food, but no customers. Small wonder that they evince little enthusiasm for these contracts; nor that, when they do accept them, they charge prices which the ordinary spectator finds exorbitant.

The ideal cricket meal is the picnic; preferably on a generous scale but, essentially, to the lunchers' taste and choice. On some grounds – Canterbury has a fine reputation in this respect – it is possible (for those who come early enough) to drive into a position from which they can watch the play from the car; and then eat and drink the provisions they have brought.

In some cases there are acceptable restaurants within a short distance of the ground; but they are exceptions and do not apply, in general, to Test grounds. Again, some few county grounds have decent catering facilities; but, while they meet the demands of county matches, they can rarely deal adequately with Test Match needs.

Travel to matches and car parking facilities raise acute problems at Test Matches. Again, county club membership – and early application for a car park pass – may overcome the problem of parking the car; though not of the long, long delay in getting away.

It cannot be over-stressed that county club membership is the only genuine way to watch first-class cricket in comfort; in discomfort its pleasures are significantly diminished.

There follow plans of the Test Match grounds as a guide to the visitor; and to help the television watcher to orientate. The notes are compiled from long, and often agonizing, experience in the hope that they may save some inconvenience.

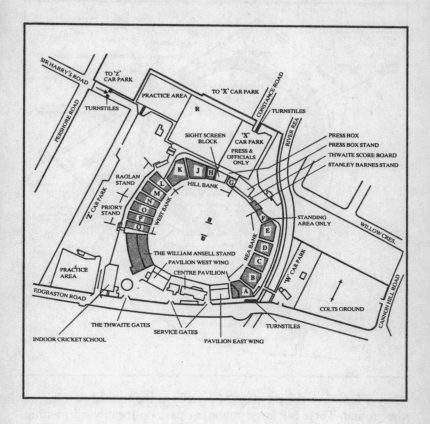

Birmingham is a motor car city; in consequence the parking facilities at Edgbaston are better than at any other Test ground. In case of difficulty or anxiety, write to the Secretary of Warwickshire CCC; they have a long and strong reputation for helpfulness and courtesy. The ground is a simple taxi drive from the city centre, but getting a cab afterwards, as from most grounds, is an acute problem. There is a good bus service. At Test Match time there are plenty of bars; and snacks are available. There are dining rooms for members, and an adequate restaurant for visitors; it is advisable to book early.

HEADINGLEY, LEEDS

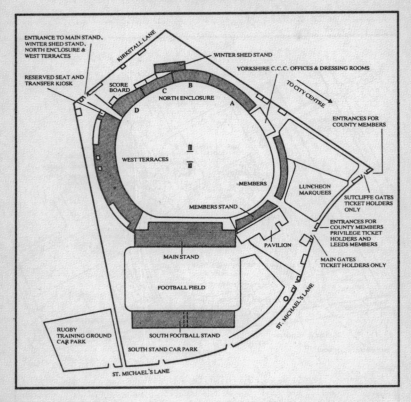

Only a few have the privilege of a place in the limited parking on the ground. There is a large public car park on the city side, within healthy walking distance of the Headingley ground. It is also possible for the early arrivals and those who know the ropes to find a place in nearby streets. Good bus service, and plenty of taxis from the city centre; getting back is the problem. Remember it is generally the most crowded of the Test grounds.

Catering is good for the members and friends of the Yorkshire club. For the rest, the bars are invariably crowded. Take a picnic lunch; it may be inconvenient to deliver it to the ground, but if that duty and the parking of the car are divided it will prove well worth while. Enjoy the picnic in the surprisingly ample space and relative comfort of the rugby league club stand, backing on to the cricket stand; or, in sunny weather, on the rugby pitch itself.

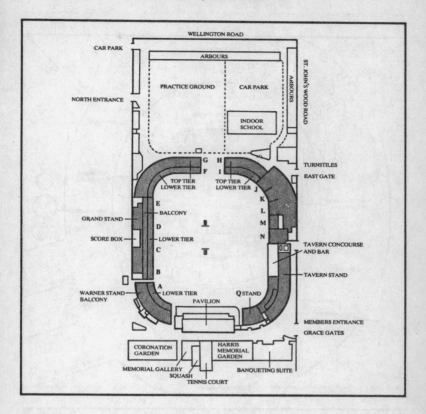

Parking is for members (of MCC) only, and not many of them; there simply is not much space in London. Better come a little early and find a place in one of the surrounding roads.

The restaurant is fair, but space is always at a premium: even two services of lunch do not feed all those who want it. There are plenty of bars, but they are always crowded. It is, though, relatively easy to find space to picnic; and those who go out to the tavern before play ends before lunch will probably be well fed.

The bus routes are sparsely served. Again, a taxi from central London is simple, but finding one for the return is impossible. The best hope is to walk down to the Edgware Road, or, further but more certain, to Baker Street. Tube to and from St John's Wood (Jubilee Line) is simplest.

THE OVAL, LONDON

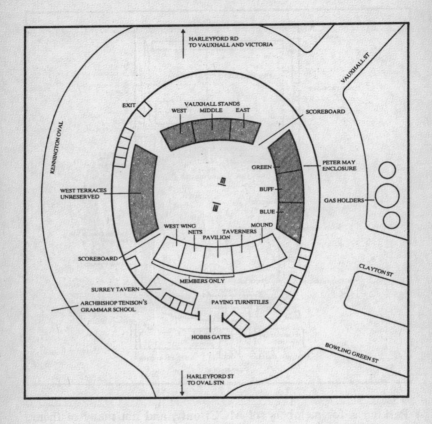

By far the best transport facilities and generally the worst parking space; even more limited than at Lord's. The tube (Northern Line), though, runs to The Oval station, only a few yards from the gates. There are plenty of bus services. Taxis to the ground are easy to find; and, over on the Kennington side of the tube station, there is a major taxi depot from which, after play, cabs are leaving minute by minute.

The ground catering is usually strained by a Test. The bars are crowded and not particularly attractive. It is worth going out to the tube, or finding a cab, and eating near Victoria or Waterloo station.

OLD TRAFFORD, MANCHESTER

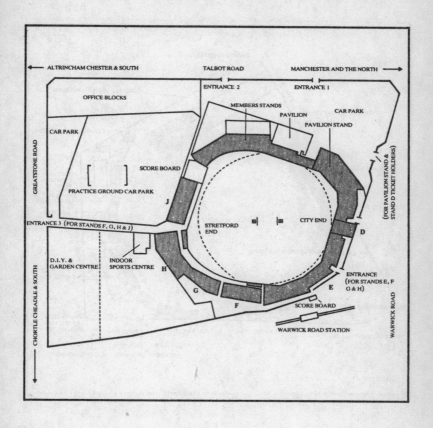

Plenty of parking on the ground; early application necessary. Not difficult, though, in the streets on the Old Stone Road side of the ground. Fair bus service from city centre; rail service to Warwick Road better still. Good, but small, restaurant on the ground (book early); relatively ample space to picnic; and a few food shops and off-licences near the ground.

TRENT BRIDGE, NOTTINGHAM

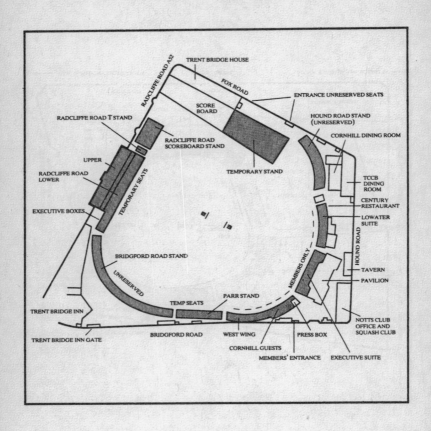

In many ways the most civilised of the Test grounds for the ordinary visitor. There is ample car parking space on the Bridgford side of the ground (furthest from the city centre); and there is a good bus service. Chances of a return taxi are remote.

The ground restaurant and special Test catering are fairly good. The Trent Bridge Hotel (locally 'the T.B.I.') is the best catering establishment on a Test ground. Reserve in advance; but they are invariably helpful. Fair space for picnics.

Chapter 6

AT THE MATCH

So, then, the spectator may settle in his seat on the ground, in the pavilion or – if he wants the best view, and without direct payment to the ground authority – in front of his television set. Equip him with a match card, scorebook if wanted, or simply a list of the players, and leave him to the divertissement.

At the start the television watcher misses atmosphere. The first ball of a Test Match – indeed, of any day's play in a Test – is one of tension. For both bowler and batsman it is a moment of nervous strain; and it is impossible for anyone present not to react to it.

The opening nowadays will virtually always be by pace bowlers from either end, because captains are not prepared to forgo the advantage of the high shine on the ball, and its assistance to swing. It was not always so. In 1909 at Edgbaston, England opened their bowling against Australia with George Hirst, fast left-arm inswing, and Colin Blythe, slow left-arm spinner: those two, bowling unchanged, put out Australia for 74; and when Australia bowled, they opened with Whitty, fast-medium left, and Macartney, slow left-arm. In the 1907 Test series in England, South Africa opened their bowling with two leg-spin-googly bowlers at Headingley – Vogler and Schwarz – and at The Oval with Vogler and Faulkner (the first and second changes, too, were googly bowlers; but that was their great period of wrist-spin). Often, too, in those days many fast bowlers – and Charles Kortright, the legendary 'fastest of them all' was among them – rubbed the new ball in the dirt to give them greater finger-purchase for their breakback.

Rule of thumb judgement on a bowler is that he is bowling well, obviously if he beats the bat, or finds the edge; less clearly if the batsman is forced to play virtually every ball; and if the batsman appears in doubt as to whether he should play back or forward.

Seam, or pace bowling

The present tendency is to preserve the shine on the ball – and, hence, its capacity for swing – as long as possible. To that end, fieldsmen will always try to return the ball on the full toss to the wicketkeeper or, if the batsmen are not running, to an intermediate fieldsman. At times, too, it seems as if everyone in the team – including the spin bowlers whose interests are not served by the practice – are diligently maintaining the shine by polishing the ball on their trousers. One capable bowler of late outswing used carefully to polish one side of the ball only, allowing the other to become rough or fluffy. His irritation when the bowler at the other end polished both sides could be quite comic.

The range of pace between seam and swing bowlers varies between the alarmingly fast and the lullingly comfortable slow-medium. It is a general truth that the fastest bowlers achieve the least swing – their pace overcomes the wind pressure on the seam which produces swing – and those of slow-medium swing most. They often do so pointlessly; producing 'banana' arcs which even the poorest batsmen can assess and play without difficulty. The most effective swing is that which happens late, immediately before the ball pitches; and, essentially, from a line which compels a stroke. Thus a good out-swinger will start along the line of the middle stump or middle-and-leg and beat, or touch, the off; the best inswinger will start about

Grip for in-swing

Grip for out-swing

Outswing and Inswing

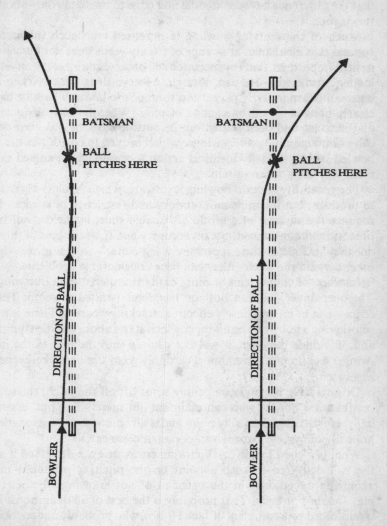

These two diagrams, in which the broken lines emphasize the line of wicket to wicket, show the course, slightly exaggerated, of:

Left   The outswinger – or outswerve – shown as swinging 'late'.

Right The inswinger – or inswerve – also shown swinging 'late'.

middle-and-off and 'do' enough to hit leg. Again, the salient fact is that the difference between middle and edge of the bat is only about two inches.

Much of the craft of bowling is practised with such intent to conceal that a batsman at a range of twenty yards does not perceive it; little hope, then, that the spectator will observe the most effectively hidden stratagems. He can, though, observe their effect. When a batsman has manifestly played too soon or too late at a ball, he has clearly been deceived by change of pace. When he has obviously played to leg and been beaten on the outside edge, he has been deceived into assuming an inswinger which proved to be a leg-cutter – bowled with a virtually identical action – or one which angled the other way off a 'green' pitch.

The generality of seam bowling is inswing, which is relatively easy to produce; but it can be monotonous and restrictive of strokes. It requires the support of a group of capable short-leg fieldsmen. Its practitioners can concentrate on accuracy and if, as the best of them do, they include in their repertoire a leg-cutter – which moves the other way off the pitch – they can pose considerable problems.

Inswing, of course, can be more easily smothered than outswing. The outswinger – as Ian Botham has demonstrated in recent Test series – can be an immensely effective attacking weapon. There is no smothering a good late outswinger which starts about middle stump; and, if it finds the edge, it will not cannon into the pad as the inswinger can do, but must almost certainly go to slip or wicketkeeper as a catch.

Given a little life and compelling some lift off the pitch, the successful seam bowler who can maintain not merely line but, essentially, length, can post a silly point and a silly mid-on and reasonably hope to compel the batsman to pop up a close catch.

What is a good length? A Victorian cricketer once described it as the ball delivered to such a point on the pitch as produced the agonizing uncertainty in the batsman of not knowing whether to play forward or back. That probably is the best of all definitions. It is reinforced by a comment of Jack Hobbs, who probably understood more about batting than anyone else: 'I don't think good batsmen get out so much to speed or swing or spin; I think most people in all cricket get out through playing back when they should play forward or forward when they should have played back.' There is more wisdom in that piece of observation than in much verbose technical analysis.

The depth of the wicketkeeper's position is not necessarily an indication of a seam bowler's pace. Of course he will stand far back to a man of great speed; or, for convenience, to the lively fast-medium; or on a lifting or unevenly paced wicket. Often, though, by standing back to one he could quite easily take over the stumps, he saves the use of a fine short-leg or a fly slip, thus allowing his captain an 'extra' man in the placings.

It is rarely indeed that a fast bowler beats batsmen by pace alone. Usually this has happened on the highest – Test – level where one country has virtually no true fast bowling in its own domestic game. That was true in England after the two World Wars, when first Gregory and MacDonald, in 1920–21 and 1921, and then Lindwall and Miller after 1945, cut down the English batting.

When Australia, in turn, fell short in that department, Tyson, especially, and Statham defeated them. That English strength might have been more apparent in that period but for the effect of the spinners, Laker, Lock and Wardle.

It is a fair generalization to say that genuinely fast bowlers have usually proved most effective in Australia; but that the fast-medium experts in swing and cut are better suited by English conditions of atmosphere and pitch.

Maurice Tate, for instance, the classic English fast-medium bowler, was widely regarded among his opponents as actually being able to gain pace off the pitch. If that is mechanically impossible, he certainly lost less than anyone else of his type; and used frequently to burst through a half-formed stroke because the batsman simply could not time him. Alec Bedser had not quite the same knack, but his swing and cut made him, like Tate, a major English asset against Australia at a time when there was little class support for them.

It has long been argued that the greatest of all bowlers was S. F. – Sydney – Barnes, the fast-medium bowler of Warwickshire, Lancashire and England but, for most of his career, Staffordshire, who played capably until his middle fifties. Clem Hill, a famous Australian opening batsman, said that, on a perfect wicket, Barnes 'could swing the new ball in and out very late; could spin from the ground; pitch on the leg-stump and miss the off'. Seen only once, and late in his career, he was a tall man with an extremely high action who made the ball move about and bounce unusually steeply.

There have been few seam bowlers of such quality; but there are many today of good control, considerable technical knowledge of their craft, who do an honest if not spectacular job. In recent years

Botham, who has added inswing to his natural outswing and has a reserve of pace in hand, has been a match-winning fast-medium bowler for England.

Another important factor in a bowler's pace – more important on the hard, relatively ungrassed pitches of Australia and West Indies – is whether, as the Australians say, he 'hits the pitch with the ball'. In English conditions it is possible for a 'skidder through' to succeed as he would never do on hard pitches; a fact that the English selectors should have observed, and had cause to regret in 1982-3.

The other weapon of the seam bowler is 'cut'; produced by hand, rather than finger, spin. Masters of it have been Alec Kennedy, Alec Bedser, George Geary, Chris Old, Phil Clift, Clive Rice.

The batsmen's response must vary according to their character and the bowler's approach. Batting against the new ball is a highly specialized matter. Against high-class opposition, the aim must generally be that of survival so long as the ball is new and moving late and sharply. There have, certainly, been attacking opening batsmen; quick in reaction and aggressive in approach. Prominent among them have been Charlie Barnett, Roy Marshall, Cyril Walters, Keith Stackpole, Harold Gimblett, all of whom attained Test status. Usually, though, the best of the opening batsmen have succeeded by virtue of sharp assessment and the ability to delay their stroke – or, equally importantly, to refrain from a stroke – until the last possible fraction of a moment. The underestimated Fred Gardner of Warwickshire was one such. Geoffrey Boycott probably has been the best of modern times in his capacity for obviating error; an ability the more impressive for the fact that he wears spectacles (or contact lenses).

Chapter 7

THE BOWLING

There now is a vast army in English cricket of practitioners of 'military medium'; bowling briskly, seam up, achieving a little movement but, above all, striving for sufficient precision to avoid punishment.

They have, to a considerable extent, replaced those spinners of former generations who either held batsmen in check by their precision (usually finger-spinners), or wrist-spinners who tossed up the ball, near or on, half-volley length, applying little or much finger- or wrist-spin and challenging the batsmen to hit them 'over the top'. Up to the outbreak of the Second World War, too, many batsmen – most, but not all, of whom did not earn their livings from the game – were happy to attempt the big hit. The more professionally conscious cricketers of today take no such risks with their living. Hence the tough, unromantic battle between the pragmatists, on either side, of 'seam up' and 'graft'.

It is often possible nowadays to watch much of a day's cricket – certainly in over-limit games – without seeing much worthwhile spin. Yet it does exist – certainly finger-spin if not wrist-spin – and at a high competitive level.

It is, though, a simple fact that it no longer plays such an important, widespread, or varied part in the game as it did until the last two decades. Of course there is spin bowling in England. Three off-spinners – Eddie Hemmings, Geoff Miller and Vic Marks – were chosen for the 1982–83 tour of Australia; while Nick Cook, slow left-arm, was desperately unlucky not to be taken. Moreover, for ten of the counties in the 1983 Championship, a spinner – finger-spinner, of course – bowled more overs than anyone else; and three were top of their counties' averages. There are, too, such highly skilled spinners as Pat Pocock – surely the best in England at the moment; the tireless David Steele; the shrewd Norman Gifford; the increasingly skilful Dipak Patel. There are not so many pairs of spinners as of old, but still Gloucestershire have the slow left-armers, David Graveney and John Childs; Middlesex, the two Test bowlers, John Emburey and Phil Edmonds.

It has been said that statistics can be made to prove anything and, if that is not quite true – and they are not always an indication of the truths of cricket – on the other hand, those who live by the score must be prepared to die by the score. Let us examine some figures. In the 1934 England–Australia series, the three Australian spinners, Bill O'Reilly, Clarrie Grimmett and Arthur Chipperfield, similar only in that they could all be described as leg-break bowlers, bowled 809.1 of the 1120.1 overs sent down for Australia in the Test series – an amazing 73% of the bowling. When Australia came here in 1981, their spin consisted of 199 of 1065 overs – 18%. In the West Indian Tests here in 1950, Ramadhin and Valentine sent down 800 of 1161 overs – 68% of the entire attack. In 1980, though, Viv Richards, who barely rates his off-breaks, and Alvin Kallicharran, bowled 43 of 886 – 5%.

Gloucestershire have long had a reputation for spin bowling, from Charlie Parker, George Dennett, Reg Sinfield, Percy Mills, through Tom Goddard and Sam Cook to David Graveney and John Childs of today. That reputation is justified, even into relatively modern times, by figures which show that, between 1946 and 1975, Tom Goddard and Monty Cranfield (most of whose cricket careers were pre-war), John Mortimore, 'Bomber' Wells, David Allen, Sam Cook, Mike Bissex, David Graveney (whose best years were still to come) and two who would have been measurable off-spinners in any other county, but who rarely got on in face of such competition – Ron Nicholls and Derek Hawkins – took, between them, 6297 wickets, an average of 314 a season. In 1950, not a remarkable summer for spinners, 2574 – 60% of the county's 4310 overs – were of finger-spin. In 1983 the figures were 1255 of 2933 – 41%. In that same 1950 season, for Yorkshire – always, and still, determined traditionalists – 2280 of 4240 overs of spin were bowled – 54%; in 1983 it was 1340 of 3047 – or 27%.

Charles Heward's statistics in Patrick Murphy's *The Spinner's Turn* show most revealingly that, in the county cricket of 1956, 51.61% of the overs bowled were of spin (41.97% of finger-spin, 9.64% of wrist-spin); in 1980 the overall figure was 36.48% of spin (35.57% finger; a pitiful 0.91% of wrist). It might be unwise to argue that this is a damaging balance *per se*. It does change the balance of the game and, in many ways, affect it as a spectacle.

Spin bowling has always offered the invitation to the attacking batsman to 'take on' the bowler. The bowler, in return, used – as he less often does today – to essay to defeat the batsman in that attempt, rather than to pin him down. If he succeeded, the result often might be a stumping. Of old, quite frequently, a county wicketkeeper might make 30 in a season: 40 was not uncommon, 50 and even over 60 has been known. Nowadays double figures is remarkable!

The employment of pace in preference to spin can be, and often is, justified on the argument of success. If a team can win by the employment of two fast bowlers, then, so the pragmatists (especially those with many fast bowlers available) argue, why not employ four (if you have them)? The recent West Indian sides, no doubt, feel themselves justified by results.

Examination of the first-class averages shows that, in 1950, 16 of the leading 20 bowlers were slow; by 1980 seven were slow and 13 fast/fast medium.

For spectators, the argument is not completely convincing. Quite apart from the type of cricket provoked by spin, pace, especially when delivered from uncontrolled – and often unnecessarily long – runs, reduces the over-rate and, hence, the amount of cricket played and watched. For example, in the 1947 series between England and South Africa, the average rate was 127 balls – 21 overs – an hour. In the England–West Indies Test of 1957, at Trent Bridge, West Indies had Frank Worrell, Roy Gilchrist, Dennis Atkinson and Garfield Sobers, as well as Ramadhin and Valentine – who, in any event, did only 30% of the bowling; England's attack, apart from Jim Laker (and five overs from Tom Graveney) consisted entirely of pace bowlers, including Fred Trueman and Brian Statham. Yet the two sides contrived to send down an average of 110 overs a day. At The Oval in 1980, the West Indies' rate was 75 balls an hour, or 75 overs a day; while Australia and England, in 1981, averaged only 14 overs an hour or 84 a day. This is pitiful commons; a cynical rate, delivered as if in contempt of the spectators.

That is one of two respects in which the appeals of the cricketing authorities on behalf of those who pay to watch have been completely disregarded by captains and players. The primary instance is that of over-rate: where the competitors obviously think – with their own good reasons – that to win is all; and, if they fret the patience of opponents and spectators in the process, that, apparently, is not a reason for their guilt.

The other, and perhaps in some ways more fundamental, regret must be that, despite all the attempts to persuade ground authorities and groundsmen to produce true fast wickets, we have an increasing crop of pitches of uneven bounce and pace; with, though, an emphasis on grass, which helps seam bowlers at the expense of the spinners.

All this adds up to a state of frustration for the idealists among county administrators. If spin bowlers do not flourish; if the fast men are given all the bowling, the kudos and all the fame, what likelihood is there that the young, always slavish imitators of their elders, will take to spin?

Let us, therefore, relish it while we may. The real drawback to the appreciation of spin, of course, is that it is not immediately, nor superficially, obvious, nor spectacular. The fast bowler can compel the intake of breath by his speed; may pluck a stump pyrotechnically from the ground; or find the edge for an acrobatic catch by the wicketkeeper or slip. The watcher, though, can only see the result of the spinner's artifice. It demands an intent observer to appreciate his subtlety to the full. For instance, how many steps did Jim Laker take to the wicket? Three? Four? Five? Six? All of them; he constantly changed his approach to defeat the batsman's timing of the ball. He had the rare ability to vary the degree of his spin; and he could appear to spin the ball hard, only for it to float on with the arm for a catch to slip or the wicketkeeper.

It is usually assumed that his greatest Test achievement was in England in 1956 when he took 46 Australian Test wickets (19 in the Old Trafford match) at an average of 9.60, and a striking rate of about one every six overs; and another 17 in Surrey's two matches against them. He, though, probably is more proud of his performance out there in 1958–59; for reasons not always obvious on the surface. The Australians were waiting for him; they claimed the pitches in England had helped him; and they swore their revenge. Laker, for his part, was not completely fit (he had to miss the Adelaide Test); and the Australians ensured that the pitches gave him no help. Yet, despite unsympathetic captaincy, in his first experience of Australian conditions, and in a losing side – defeated by the four Australian 'chuckers' – he finished top of the English bowling both in aggregate and average for the Tests. Denied the pitches on which he could exploit his aptitude for quick spin, he relied almost entirely on flight and variation; linked to field-placings of his own planning. Thus wide is the range and, therefore, the field of appreciation of the finger-spinner. He, though, is peculiarly an English type. It used to be said, falsely, but, for Australian batsmen, valuably, that English off-spinners could never succeed in Australia. That, though, is, arguably, traditionally the peak of the English professional's skill.

Many of them, too, were masters of 'curve' or 'swerve' as distinct from swing. While it may well be that Sydney Barnes procured the same effect at some pace, this is generally the domain of the spinner. The ball which will turn from leg – whether bowled by a right-arm wrist-spinner or left-arm finger-spinner – will tend to dip in to the batsman; similarly, the ball spun to turn in to the bat will float away in the air. Ian Johnson, the Australian, achieved far more away-float than spin; but Fred Titmus and Ray Illingworth were major artificers in this skill. Spin the ball enough and it will curve through the air before turning in the opposite direction.

Such men – left-arm or right – as Wilfred Rhodes, Colin Blythe, Bobby Peel, Johnnie Briggs, Hedley Verity, Charlie Parker, Tom Goddard, Fred Titmus, David Allen – reached high peaks of artifice. So, too, did others who rarely, if ever, attained Test status because of the immense wealth of English cricket in this department for more than a century.

To watch such a man as Horace Hazell, who never played a Test, wheeling away to precise length and line, but with subtle variations not to be detected from the ring, was to be lulled into a rhythm of cricket as beguiling as that he was creating – with no ultimately restful intent – for the batsman. The very arc of the finger-spinner's flight is all but hypnotic; and if it is ever lost, cricket, and the watching of it, will be inestimably the poorer.

Wrist-spin

It may be argued that, if finger-spin is characteristically English, wrist-spin is the Australian form. In that direction, Bernard Bosanquet – the inventor of the googly – the spectacular spinner, Alan Steel, Eric Hollies, Len Braund, 'Tich' Freeman, Ian Peebles and Johnnie Wardle – who, when he departed from his orthodox slow left-arm could bowl wrist-spin in quite masterly fashion – would dispute Australian eminence. Nevertheless, Australia maintained the tradition more determinedly through the post-war period. From every point of view – spin, control, variation, tactical sense, flight – there has barely been a better leg-break bowler than Bruce Dooland; while Richie Benaud took more wickets than any other wrist-spinner in Test cricket. South Africa, too, over a brief, but amazingly rich period, exploited the leg-break and googly with shattering effect. Even there, and in Australia, though, its use has waned in recent years.

Leg-Spin and Off-Spin

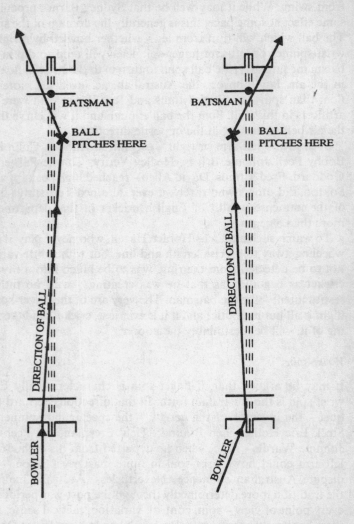

These two diagrams, in which the broken lines emphasize the line of wicket to wicket, show the course of:

Left The leg-break (right-arm leg-spinner, left-arm finger-spinner or the googly of the left-arm wrist-spinner).

Right The off-break (right-arm finger-spinner, the googly of the right-arm wrist-spinner; or the stock ball of the left-arm wrist-spinner).

Grip for leg-spin: as seen by the batsman

Grip for off-spin

*Grip for leg-spin: as seen from
behind the bowler*

This decline can but impair and impoverish cricket. Not only is the game deprived of an important traditional facet, and an ingredient of entertainment; but one which 'loosened up the game' and speeded its action, by encouraging attacking batting and quick scoring; and also generally produced a high striking rate – frequency of wickets in relation to overs bowled.

Its neglect, not only in English cricket, but, quite strikingly, by English cricketers, is one of the most disappointing aspects of the game in the past decade here. Both the first and the second places in the records for the most wickets taken and the most balls bowled in a season are held by A. P. – 'Tich' – Freeman, the Kent leg-spin and googly bowler. In 1928 he took 304 wickets in 1976 overs (average 18.05); and, in 1933, 298 in 2039, at 15.26. There are thirteen instances of a man taking more than 250 wickets in a single season, six of them standing to Freeman's credit, and he took 100 wickets in every season from 1920 to 1936. Indeed, in the entire history of cricket only one man – Wilfred Rhodes – took more than Freeman's 3776.

Freeman was often said to bowl a top spinner: certainly he often had that effect. It is, though, obviously impossible to bowl a 'pure' top spinner unless the wrist were a ball swivel. His top spinner, in other words, was a leg-break or – more often – a googly which 'didn't'. For that reason it was the more effective: gathering pace, going straight through and giving him many lbws.

English wrist-spin, however, by no means ended with Freeman. It has almost invariably been leg-break and googly bowling. The similar left-arm wrist-spin – in effect an off-break, as its googly is a leg-break – to the right-handed batsman, has been almost solely an Australian fashion. Maurice Leyland, and his father before him, are generally credited with originating it, and certainly with christening it the Chinaman – 'because it's mysterious'. They regarded it with a certain amount of mirth – but bowled it with some effect: while Johnnie Wardle, when he chose to employ it instead of his usual orthodox slow left-arm, was a positive master in the style. The three outstanding practitioners, though, were the Australians, 'Chuck' Fleetwood-Smith, Jack Walsh and George Tribe, of whom the last two came to England and played with considerable success for Leicestershire and Northamptonshire respectively. Indeed, Jack Walsh took 100 wickets in a season seven times (174 in 1948) between 1946 and 1953; Tribe eight times between 1952 and 1959. Each of them, too, took the record aggregate of wickets in a season for those counties: Tribe 175 and Walsh 170. Meanwhile, another Australian, John McMahon, joined Surrey as a left-arm wrist-spinner; but he changed to orthodox left-arm when he moved to Somerset.

Three wrist-spinners took 100 wickets in the English season of 1956 – and four in 1957. In the first case they were Roly Jenkins and two Australians in Bruce Dooland and George Tribe; in the second, Eric Hollies, Tribe and Dooland again, and Gamini Goonasena from Ceylon. In the first case, though, Tommy Greenhough, Bill Greensmith, Eric Hollies and Doug Wright (as well as Colin McCool and Gamini Goonasena) took over 50. Tommy Greenhough (Lancashire) took 100 wickets in both 1959 and 1960. From then on, though, the decline has been sharp and tragic.

The last serious English leg-break and googly bowler – at least the last chosen for a Test – was Robin Hobbs of Essex. In 1970, he sent down 625.5 overs in the County Championship. That was more than the total number bowled in the entire County Championship of 1982. The figure in that instance was 618.3. Its most surprising facet, though, is that, of that 618.3, only 136 were bowled by English-born cricketers. Of the other 482.3, Asif Din, the Ugandan Asian of Warwickshire, bowled far more than anyone else – 252.1; the two Pakistanis, Javed Miandad and Sadiq Mohammad, both, by coincidence, bowled 101.4; and Russell McCool (son of Colin McCool), the young Somerset-born Australian, 27. Between them,

W. G. Grace, described on the Grace Gates at Lord's simply as
'The Great Cricketer', was the eminent Victorian of sport,
the creator of modern batsmanship, and breaker of records
and bowlers. (MCC)

Australia's most popular cricketer: the immortal
Victor Trumper jumps out to drive.
(The George Beldam Collection)

K.S. Ranjitsinhji (LEFT), or 'Ranji', the supreme exponent of
the leg glance and, according to Gilbert Jessop, 'the most
brilliant figure' during the Golden Age of Cricket.
Gilbert Jessop (RIGHT), the most consistent big hitter in the
history of the game, demonstrates one of his most prolific
strokes, the pull. (The George Beldam Collection)

Jack Hobbs, who scored more
runs (61,237) than anyone else
in the history of cricket,
succeeded W. G. Grace as the
finest batsman in the world,
and bridged the years between
the Grace and Bradman eras.
'The Master' had a complete
range of strokes, including the
off-drive (TOP LEFT); the hook
(TOP RIGHT); and the leg glance
(RIGHT). (Press Association)

Wally Hammond, one of the three greatest English batsmen:
noted in particular for the power and majesty of his cover
driving. (H.H. Fishwick/David Frith Collection)

Donald Bradman, who averaged 99.94 in his 80 Test innings,
dominated the cricket world between 1930 and 1948 by quite
imperious batting. The cut (LEFT) and the pull (RIGHT) were
just two of the many strokes he played with complete mastery.
(Central Press/Press Association)

Spectators warmed to Denis Compton as instinctively and as happily as he batted. His performance in 1947, when he scored a record 3816 runs including 18 hundreds, was the statistical peak of a career which lasted from 1936 to 1958. His hallmark was the sweep (ABOVE); and he played the cover drive (RIGHT) to perfection. (Sport & General/ Press Association)

ABOVE

Two studies in defence: Trevor Bailey, whose resistance provided constantly crucial balance to the winning English teams of the 1950s; and Geoffrey Boycott, England's anchor man for most of the time from 1964 to 1981. (Sport & General/Patrick Eagar)

LEFT

Peter May, England's consistently outstanding batsman of the 1950s, was a classically upstanding stroke-player. His driving was superb, particularly wide of mid-on. (Sport & General)

David Gower's late cut (ABOVE) and Viv Richards's square cut (RIGHT): characteristic strokes of two of the most talented batsmen of modern times. (Patrick Eagar)

Greg Chappell, always strong on the leg side, hooking with
innately perfect timing. (Adrian Murrell/All Sport)

those four took 34 of the 42 wickets to fall to this type of bowling.

This happened, too, in a season when Abdul Qadir of Pakistan was to be seen, in action and on television, bowling the leg-break and googly with such consummate skill as to baffle most English batsmen. In 12 matches of the short Pakistan tour, he bowled 452 overs and took 57 wickets at 20.82; the other leg-spinner in the Pakistani party, Wasim Raja, took nine wickets in 117.4 overs. Since Robin Hobbs, too, the most active leg-break bowlers in the English game have been Pakistanis – the brothers Mushtaq Mohammad and Sadiq Mohammad; and Intikhab Alam.

Nevertheless, Pakistani, Indian and – though decreasingly – Australian cricketers continue to demonstrate the art to the interest and entertainment of watchers. The flight of the leg-break can be puzzling, especially when it is spun hard, with the ball heavy against the third finger in preparation for the delivery swing, and then a full whip of the wrist. Then it will curve in towards the legs of the right-hand batsman; but it will also, often, dip disconcertingly. Arthur Mailey used to delight in floating the ball in to the line of the leg stump and making it whip away outside the off. He also, though, twice bowled out Jack Hobbs in Test Matches with full tosses which 'dipped' steeply as he went through with his stroke. Another indication of the change in the times is the fact that both batsman and bowler laughed.

The googly, of course, is historically accepted as an English invention. Others may have achieved it earlier but by accident or design without being given the credit for it. However it is certain that B. J. T. – Bernard – Bonsanquet, the all-rounder who played for Oxford University, Middlesex and England between 1898 and 1919, discovered it in a game called 'twisti twosti' in which a soft ball is spun on to a table with intent to beat the opponent by the turn. Bosanquet found he could deceive his opponent by making a ball bowled out of the back of the right hand turn the 'wrong' way. Formerly a fast-medium bowler, he perfected the delivery to such a peak as to surprise – even astonish – the best batsmen of his time.

Simply enough, what, from his hand action, appeared to be a leg-break proved to be an off-break. Mixed in with actual leg-breaks, its effect recalled Nyren's phrase of Lamborn, the Hambledon 'little shepherd' who, in the eighteenth century, first exploited the off-break: 'Egad this new trick of his so bothered (the opposing batsmen) that they tumbled out one after another as if they had been picked off by a rifle corps.'

In more concrete terms, Bosanquet decisively tilted the England–Australia series of 1903–04 and 1905. He could be most amusing about his creation, which he described as 'not unfair, only immoral'. He recalled its first first-class victim – Sam Coe of Leicestershire – who had made 98 when he was 'stumped off a fine specimen which bounced four times'; 'William Gunn stumped when nearer my wicket than his own'; Arthur Shrewsbury complaining that 'it wasn't fair'. Bosanquet's immortality lies in the Australian name for the googly – the 'Bosie'.

When the South African, R. O. Schwarz, was playing for Middlesex he studied Bosanquet's method, and returned to his own country to teach the trick there. By the time the English touring team of 1905–06 arrived the Africans had five capable googly bowlers who effectively won them the rubber by four matches to one. It is, perhaps, the key to the googly that Schwarz himself could only bowl a googly – but not the leg-break at all; and yet he still beat batsmen who knew it. It can be almost hypnotic when batsmen are not truly accustomed to it; and their spontaneous response is to play it as a leg-break. The best players of the time did it; even Victor Trumper; and Tom Hayward was virtually put out of Test cricket by his inability to play it. It is interesting to note that Jack Hobbs, who so completely mastered the South African googly bowlers in 1909–10 as to score 539 runs at 67.37, always said that he did not attempt to read their hands but played them strictly 'off the pitch'.

Even with the passage of some eighty years, it remains a considerable weapon in the hands of someone who can bowl it accurately. The pragmatists of the present day have worked out their 'percentages'. They estimate that the average wrist-spinner will bowl one bad ball an over; if they can hit that for four and live through the other five, they are showing a batting profit. As a corollary to that point of view, Yorkshire, the ultimate realists of the cricketing economy, historically regarded leg-spin as 'not business'. Indeed, they never included a regular wrist-spinner in their team until Eddie Leadbetter (1949–56), and have not done so since. Still, though, when a Chandrasekhar or an Abdul Qadir comes along, he is always likely to conquer; and to delight the interested watcher.

The report, at the end of the 1982 season, that Abdul Qadir might join Kent made potentially exciting news. Not only does he add to the interest – indeed, the excitement – of watching cricket; but as a team-mate he would have been an example and encouragement for Derek Aslett – the chief English leg-spinner of 1983 with 37 overs and three wickets for 218. Meanwhile Kim Barnett of Derbyshire, of whom there had been such high hopes, bowled himself for only three overs and figures of none for 13.

All this could represent the passing of a tradition of English cricket, for, if there is no adequate coach of any form of cricket, there are hardly likely to be motivated or adequately equipped pupils.

Lob bowling

Lob, or under-arm bowling, was the earliest form of bowling (round-arm was not legalized until 1828; over-arm not until 1864) and it is still permissible today. The bowler must, though, inform the umpire that he intends to bowl it – as he must of any method he adopts.

There is reliable contemporary evidence that the early under-arm bowlers achieved not only considerable spin but also swing ('bias') and even pace – 'How it was that those balls acquired the velocity they did by this mode of delivery I never could comprehend' wrote Nyren of the Hambledon bowler, David Harris. There were those who protested that the 1828 admission of 'the new throwing bowling' would ruin the skills of the game; and certainly many skilful and successful cricketers practised it until far into the nineteenth century.

The most recent instance, of course, was by the Australian Trevor Chappell who, on his captain's instructions, bowled an under-arm 'grub' as the last ball of an Australia–New Zealand over-limit match when New Zealand wanted only six runs to tie. Generally in recent years the method has been employed as a gesture of annoyance at a batsman's obdurate defence.

The skill persisted, however, and George Simpson-Hayward (who, playing for Cambridge University and Worcestershire between 1899 and 1914, took 510 wickets at 21.46) was good enough to be chosen for Gentlemen v Players; and, in the five Tests in South Africa in 1909–10, had the good figures of 23 wickets at 18.26. He gave the ball less air than most of his type and, unusually for a right-arm lob-bowler, turned it, not from leg but – extremely sharply – from the off. The last man to bowl lobs habitually and seriously at first-class level was T. J. Malony who in 1921 appeared in two matches for Surrey and took four wickets for 89 runs.

Chapter 8

FIELDING AND WICKETKEEPING

Whatever criticisms or suggestions of deterioration may be levelled at other departments of modern cricket, there can be no question that fielding has improved. The ultimate stimulus was provided by the over-limit game but progress had already been observed for some years.

It can be suggested that the earliest specialist settings were for George Hirst's fast left-arm: certainly a highly concentrated leg trap was set by Somerset and Worcestershire for Bill Gresswell's slowish, and Fred Root's faster, inswing during the early nineteen-twenties. There was, too, the leg-side concentration first employed by Arthur Carr and then by Douglas Jardine for what was called the 'body-line' tactic of Harold Larwood and Bill Voce in 1932–33. Then came more intense aggressive fields for both fast and slow bowlers of Yorkshire, and Tom Goddard's off-spin for Gloucestershire.

At the end of the Second World War the Australian Services team toured England and included a repatriated prisoner of war of the Russians, Keith Carmody, who returned to New South Wales and then moved on to coach and captain Western Australia. He was one of the most thoughtful of cricketers. Australia, of course, had long had a high reputation for fielding; and Carmody planned his operations with skill. He introduced a packed, eight-man, close – or 'umbrella' – setting for new-ball bowlers which became known as the 'Carmody field'. Many variations of this were employed. The most strikingly successful early example of an attacking field, though, was that of Glamorgan when they won the Championship of 1948 under Wilfred Wooller. They were by no means the strongest batting or bowling side in the country, but the outstanding close catching of Arnold Dyson, Allan Watkins, Phil Clift, Gilbert Parkhouse and Wooler himself; plus the wicketkeeping of Haydn Davies and the brilliance in the deep of Willie Jones, to the off-spin of John Clay and Len Muncer and the slow left-arm of Stan Trick, took them to the title.

Some highly expert cricket minds focused on field settings for Yorkshire and Middlesex but, with the start of the over-limit game, Lancashire, under Jack Bond, became probably the finest fielding side England has ever known. As a result, although they had won only one (shared) County Championship title since 1934, between 1969 and 1976 they won the Gillette Cup four times, were twice losing finalists; and won the John Player League twice.

Their progress did not pass unnoticed among other counties. The overall result has been an all-round rise in the standard of fielding. It is now uneconomic, and all but impossible, to include in a team – and hide in the field – those slow movers and non-benders who, until relatively recently, a number of counties found it worthwhile to 'carry' in the field for their batting or bowling value.

Fielding is, in some ways, the most spontaneous of cricketing skills. Anyone who has watched Clive Lloyd or Derek Randall at cover point; Ian Botham at slip; Mike Gatting and Phil Edmonds near the bat; or Chris Cowdrey anywhere, must appreciate that. It is, however, possible to become a good – though not a great – fieldsman by practice, diligence and concentration. Two fine batsmen, Sir Jack Hobbs and Geoffrey Boycott, were both rebuked for poor fielding in their early days in the first-class game. Sir Jack practised so determinedly as to become one of the finest cover-points in the world; and Boycott, despite the handicap of deficient eyesight, made himself into a conscientious outfielder and a monumentally safe catcher.

The standard of fielding is of immense psychological importance in competitive cricket. Where it is high, bowlers feel themselves well supported, and therefore more confident than when they are let down by dropped catches or sloppy ground fielding. Nothing spurs a bowler quite so much from an apparently unrewarding plod as a blinding catch of a half-chance. The fact of an entire team being brisk, on its toes, and eager gives it corporate drive and tends to give it dominance over the batting side. It enables a captain, too, to put opponents under pressure.

There are some sound rules about ground fieldsmen getting their legs – feet – bodies – behind the ball; catchers judging the flight of the ball, keeping down, watching the bat, and so on. Sustained good fielding, though, depends on certainty, whether from well-drilled discipline or the most sudden reflex reaction which results in a brilliant catch; and basically, certainly, stems from unremitting concentration.

Wicketkeeping is undoubtedly the most taxing job in cricket, demanding a higher standard of stamina, certainty – in effect infallibility – than of anyone else on the field. Hence the old adage among those responsible for selection – always pick the best wicket-keeper. The mistake of taking the second-best because he can bat better than his superior as a keeper has lost many a match; once, perhaps, a Test series. It has been said, with some truth, that wicket-keepers are born, not made. Batsmen, fieldsmen, slow bowlers and fast bowlers have been created from unexpected, if not unpromising, material. Wicketkeeping, however, with its demand on assessment of a ball of which he must almost certainly lose sight – perhaps twice – in its flight, is a peculiar knack which many people have found impossible to acquire.

The speed in diving for a catch, or making a stumping, of the great wicketkeeper is the more impressive when, as is often over-looked, he has been six hours in the field. In that time he has been 'taking' – in preparation and the mind – every ball bowled; getting up to the stumps to take returns from the field, often from a deep position to a fast bowler.

The standard of wicketkeeping in English cricket has generally been professionally high. Today, under the stimulus of competition, it probably is higher than it has ever been in respect of keeping to pace and swing bowling; and even, which is not easy, to flat, pushed-through spin. It is not so high in relation to stumpings, largely because, as has already been argued, the types of bowling which produce the opportunities for them simply are not practised as they once were. Leslie Ames of Kent, keeping wicket to 'Tich' Freeman, the tiny, slow, wrist-spin bowler of the inter-war period, enjoyed high success in that direction. In the 1932 season he made 64 stump-ings; in 1928, 52; in 1929, 48. Hugo Yarnold of Worcestershire made 47 in 1949. In the 1983 season, by contrast, the highest tally was 'Jack' Russell's 17, followed by Bobby Parks's, Roger Tolchard's and David Humphries's nine; five regular county wicketkeepers made less than four.

The wicketkeeper, though, can only do what the bowlers and the conditions of play allow him to do. Nowadays, with the increased thought devoted to equipment and light gear and, above all, the increased athleticism, fitness, mobility and the speed of movement, the work of the men who stand back and hurl themselves vast distances to make catches – and especially to scoop up a catch falling short of the slips – could hardly be bettered. Add to all this the fact that the really good wicketkeeper is completely unobtrusive, unless he makes a mistake. You ought not to notice him: in other words, his skill should have the air of inevitability. Thus the outcricketing weapon to the hand of the modern captain is sharper than ever before.

Chapter 9

CAPTAINCY

The captain of a cricket team has more wide-ranging, profound, onerous and unforeseeable duties than a leader in any other sport. Mike Brearley, the extremely successful modern example of the outstanding captain, posed the problem admirably when he wrote in *Wisden* for 1982: 'The captain of a county cricket team is, all at once, managing director, union leader and pit-face worker. He has almost total charge of the daily running of the concern; he is the main, if not the only, representative of the work force in the board-room (i.e. on the committee) and he has to field, bat and maybe bowl. He conducts the orchestra and he performs; perhaps on the front deck of the violins or as second tambourine (it varies; I've been both). Consequently it is hard to play God, to read the Riot Act about carelessness or incompetence, when one throws one's own wicket away or plays ineptly – if not today, tomorrow or yesterday. Any conscience on this score can inhibit one's own play; the captain oscillates between pawkiness – being over-anxious about careless-ness – and, aware of the tendency to criticise others for slow scoring, an inappropriate desperation for quick runs.' It could not be better, more humanly, nor more perceptively put. There they are: all the horns of the classic dilemma of the man who aspires – or is ordered – to captain a cricket team.

Clearly the man who succeeds needs a modicum of luck. He needs much more. Of old – indeed, not long ago in some counties – the captain wielded almost feudal power; his decision was unquestion-able. Now, though, with the breakdown of the former gentleman-player distinction, the position is different. Players no longer hesitate to doubt, question or even openly criticize a captain. Formerly, too, there was a certain confidentiality about the counsels, discussions or disagreements within a cricket team. Nowadays, increasingly, the media demand explanations; and the captain who is not forthcoming may well find himself pilloried.

On the non-defensive side the good captain can, as the current term is, 'motivate' his players – if he has the right personality. The

England–Australia Test series of 1981 is the classic example. After Lord's, Brearley took over a side which had lost one match, made an unhappy draw of a second; and wore a sadly defeated look. His influence changed the character of the team. The same men who had looked beaten put on a look of confidence and – thanks to some all but miraculous cricket by Botham and Willis – became runaway winners of the series. That, of course, was the most striking example of a captaincy transformation in cricket history. There were many contributory factors for which it would be impossible to give Brearley – or, in some instances, his players – the credit; and he and they, for their parts, would not demand it. The fact remains that, at bottom, that team and its performances were changed by a change of captain.

While captaincy in the field must, of course, be informed and based on experience, much is intuitive. The captain feels that he is losing grip; that the opposing batsmen are beginning to dominate. On a good wicket, once all the bowlers have been used, and the ball is worn, there is no obvious bowler to use. That is when the captain needs both luck, the knack of happy guessing and that extra sense which good captains do, in fact, often develop.

Style in captaincy must be a matter of character. Of the most successful, Douglas Jardine was tough, inflexible, autocratic. Don Bradman led largely by the example of his batting, but also with the experience of many years of astute, unwinking, objectively cool study of play and players. Richie Benaud was a flair captain: essentially a quick-thinking, confident cricketer, prepared to take on the opposition with a belief that he could win; though, as must be observed, he had the players to reinforce that impression. Ray Illingworth and Len Hutton were two Yorkshiremen: deep students of the game; aware of every trick in the hand; and unrelenting in their grip on a match; holding on, yielding not the slightest advantage, waiting for the sight of the opening to win; and then throwing in everything. There was, about their leadership and tactics, a certain sameness; but, importantly, they always perceived the salient tactical points, and never got the priorities wrong.

At county level, Wilfred Wooller and Stuart Surridge were the drivers, urging their team on with as many imprecations as words of encouragement. Some teams, like those of Yorkshire between the wars, almost literally captained themselves, every professional knowing what to do and when to do it.

Two modern factors have completely changed the status and

significance of the captain. The first is, clearly, the extent of sponsors' prize money. Thus the captain holds within his hand a significant proportion of all his players' potential earnings: far greater than that of the talent money at stake until relatively recently. This places on his shoulders a responsibility which the players themselves do not want. He now must satisfy them, as well as his committee, or have trouble on his hands. Secondly, he is the one who must carry the burden of adjusting to the changed tempo of play. So long as cricket proceeded at an established and accustomed rhythm, the deeply established thought-processes of the experienced players remained valid. The over-limit game – not necessarily the villain of the piece but certainly the major factor of change, whether for good or ill – altered all that. Now captains must take upon themselves adjustments to switches from the completely different shape of games between close of play in a Championship match on Saturday – through a John Player fixture on Sunday – and back to the three-day tempo on Monday.

This violent upset of pattern is as much as most men can tolerate in terms of play alone. They become increasingly prepared to yield decision to the captain.

In many cases, however, the captain himself does not relish the dichotomy. That was in part the reason for the gradual introduction of the team manager. Kent were the first county to make this decision; and with generally happy results. They have been followed by Lancashire, Yorkshire, Surrey and Nottinghamshire; while in Leicestershire and Glamorgan there have been second – and not necessarily secondary – influences. So far most of the divisions of responsibility seem to have occurred without undue problems. In fact, the separation of worries has often appeared healthy. Captains with present-day problems of urgency may well be grateful to be relieved of long-term decisions on matters like contracts, recruiting, engagements, re-engagements and dismissal. Yet these are matters of ultimate importance to any captain who expects a long-term continuance with a county; and on mature consideration he will hardly be willing to surrender his interest.

The fact, as has been argued from the start, is that the ordinary day-to-day captaincy of a county team is stressful enough for any man who will field, bat, and perhaps bowl, as well. It is easy to forget not only that he cannot relax in the field because he must be observing and directing the course of play; but also that he cannot relax, either, during his own team's innings. He needs to watch the progress of his batsmen; it may be that a collapse – or even a sudden access to dominance – justifies a change of batting order. One extremely good England Test player, who also proved a sympathetic and shrewd county captain, once said: 'Captaincy finished me; before then, once I got out, I used to get a sleep while the rest of the side were batting; when I didn't get that relaxation I just felt so damned tired I don't think I was half the player afterwards.' It is possible, too, to point to a marked number of good cricketers whose playing performances went off, particularly in the first season after appointment to the captaincy, and often for longer.

The chapter on captaincy in Prince Ranjitsinhji's *Jubilee Book of Cricket* – incidentally almost solely written by C. B. Fry – is both sage and readable. At the end the author says, on the subject of declarations, 'It is a difficult point to give advice upon. The choice is between the dashing and the safe game. On the whole, I think, it is best to go for the gloves' (typical C. B. Fry language). 'Unfinished matches are an abomination. It is almost worth giving the other side just a chance of winning whenever it is possible to do so, purely for the sake of sport and a close finish . . . It is on general grounds better to have tried and lost than never to have tried at all.' That advice would hardly be accepted by a Test captain today. In the over-limit game there is no choice: the game is played to an arbitrary formula so that, except in such weather conditions that not even the sketchiest result is possible, every game is played to a finish. In Test Matches, chances are not taken. The last international captain to declare and give the other side a chance was Garfield Sobers, captain of West Indies against England at Port-of-Spain in 1968. After three drawn matches he declared and set England 215 to win in 165 minutes; and they got them. Many critics set up an outcry against him; none more loudly than those who for years had called for bold captaincy and an end to safety-first draws in Test Matches. They even forgot to give him credit for failing by only a single wicket to win the following Test almost off his own bat.

The good captain will have a sound knowledge of his opponents. At any level, if he has not played against them as a team or against their more important players as individuals, he will make intelligent enquiries about them. Thus he can advise and handle his bowlers, place his field and counsel his batsmen. Such information can decide a match. Ideally, he will have a sound and workable plan in mind before each innings starts; but he will be wise enough not to adhere to it slavishly but to keep an open mind, and to be flexible to the extent of rethinking his strategy in light of unexpected developments. He will not make changes in the bowling for the sake of change; he will not run dully through all his change bowling when he might with greater advantage revert to his best bowler(s). Similarly he will not overbowl the most penetrative of them, but keep him sufficiently fresh to kill off the opposing tail.

Study of opponents is important. Some batsmen flinch from pace, and will therefore be plied with fast bowling. Some batsmen fret if they are pinned down so that they cannot break their duck. In that case a pair of accurate bowlers may worry them into self-destruction. Again, some bowlers are disturbed, and cannot bowl their best, when faced by a left-hander. Others find it difficult to maintain accuracy when they bowl to a combination of right-hander and left. Countless such instances arise for exploitation. No captain knows them all; the good captain, by study, ascertains as many of them as he can.

The critical spectator will notice whether a captain is purposeful; if he maintains the flow of the match; if he catches the eyes of his players frequently enough not to have to shout to them, but can make a field-change unobtrusively.

The wise captain will not spurn advice, but will take it quietly – ideally, like any rebuke he may have to offer, in the privacy of the dressing room; he will maintain discipline by personal contact.

Other factors emerge. A captain is his own, and his team's, public relations officer. An early arrival at the ground; courtesy to the opposing captain, players, umpires, scorers and staff; and a polite farewell are the mark of a good skipper at any level of play. On tour, the burdens are the same, merely heavier.

Much of the profundity – technical, cerebral and human – of cricket is vested in every captain who attempts to discharge his responsibilities conscientiously. It is a demanding, even sapping, task.

Chapter 10

BATTING

So, after all the forces which assault it, to the fourth 'straight stick' and the man who wields it in defence of the other three. The purpose of batting is to score runs; though, to do that as effectively as possible, the batsman must be able to defend his wicket, and to avoid the other nine methods of getting out listed on pages 7 and 8. Cricket is a team game, and most teams need a sheet-anchor, defensive batsman for security.

The strokes of the batsman may be divided between defensive and attacking; between forward strokes when the batsman's weight is thrown mainly on to the front (in the case of a right-handed batsman, the left) foot; or the back (or right) foot. W. G. Grace always used to argue that when a ball beat him (generally, presumably, by its teasing length) he played half-cock, that is, neither forward nor back. That is a comment not to be ignored, but not unduly to affect this discussion.

The best batsmen have always been accomplished off both the front foot and the back, playing from either according to the length of the ball. No great batsman is solely a back-foot or a front-foot player; though the brilliant West Indian, George Headley, probably played forward less than anyone else of comparable ability.

The essence of defensive – and most attacking – strokes is that they are played with a perpendicular – straight – bat. On the other hand, certain profitable and orthodox strokes, such as the pull or the hook ('pulled' from any length, 'hooked' if short) which send the ball through the leg-side; and the cut, late or square, which sends it through the arc from fine to forward of square on the off-side, are played with a bat at an angle varying between the mildly slanting and the horizontal.

Of the normal strokes it is fair to say that the on-drive is the most difficult to play; the cut probably the most delicate; the off-drive and the cover drive the most handsome; the lofted straight drive, the hook and the full-blooded square cut, the most spectacular.

Any good coaching book will describe the strokes in detail and indicate possible flaws in their execution. That is a matter for the technician. What the books cannot describe is the improvisation. Sir Donald Bradman was always interested in this aspect of batting. Most sound batsmen, he asserted, could play the text-book strokes; but how many could invent a stroke when they suddenly found themselves stranded? He was wont, then, to describe going down the pitch to a fastish bowler in grade cricket: the ball swung violently away to the full reach of his bat and he played a slash, undercutting the ball which curved away over the (short) third-man boundary for six. The bowler apostrophized him in good Sydney terms for 'a fluky bastard'. Bradman answered, 'You bowl it again and I'll do it again' – and closed the story with 'and he did and I did'. Among modern batsmen no one has improvised more splendidly creatively than Barry Richards who, apparently, did not enjoy it.

Much of true appreciation of batting, however, lies in the manner of the batsman. Style needs no definition: ease – even elegance – of movement must be apparent to any watcher; nothing is more felicitous than the unhurried flow of a poised batsman into, and through, a stroke which seems, without violence, to charm – almost chasten – the fast ball to the boundary. That is compounded of several ingredients, most of which may be imparted by teaching but which, in the best instances, have been instinctive. Great batsmen as different – yet as similar – as Sir Jack Hobbs and Sir Garfield Sobers, for instance, on their own testimony, never received a moment's coaching. Yet, except when, through desire, they chose to improvise – and had the genius to do so – they could both be as orthodoxly correct as the sternest purist could ask. The first ingredient of a good stroke, no doubt, is early reading of the ball: identification of its pace, spin and, above all, its length. That early evaluation is undoubtedly the basis of the lack of hurry which has always marked the great batsman. The parts of this judgement are not the same; nor do they necessarily go hand in hand. The ability to pick the ball up early in flight is a matter of eyesight and speed of reaction. Assessment, though, depends on ball sense, which is an entirely different matter. It is the basis of ability at all ball games except, perhaps, rugby football. It is the one completely incommunicable competence of them all, yet, in many people, evaluation of the behaviour of a ball, how it will fall, bounce or turn, is instinctive. That early identification enables the batsman to move into position to deal with the ball. Once his feet are in the right place, the stroke becomes relatively easy to play; if he is a good player it will automatically be the ideal stroke, played at the right point.

All this is, perhaps, an overelaborate description of what is, for some, a purely instinctive response to someone bowling a ball at them. The second ingredient is timing; which may be described as the application of maximum force by minimum exertion. Without it, the ball can be hammered into the ground, skied or merely stunned. With it, it will go sweetly, almost startlingly, away. The final ingredient is placing which also, in the great,. has seemed all but automatic.

Over the years there has been a constant battle between bat and ball. As batsmen dominate, so bowlers evolve a fresh tactic. Whether it be the googly, inswing to a leg-side field, or the bouncer, it is, in its turn, mastered. In the short term, too, this applies.

Contrary to the apparent – certainly the voiced – opinions of some spectators who obviously have never played the game, bowlers do not bowl for the purpose of becoming batsmen's chopping blocks. Good bowlers have from time to time tied down the best of batsmen.

None of these attributes, however, is of practical value unless the batsman can build an innings; play himself in, gradually – or rapidly – extend his range of strokes within sensed control; and continue, never relaxing concentration sufficiently to make the two-inch error between middle and edge of bat, playing the innings necessary. Since cricket is essentially a team game, an innings is only assessable in terms of the team's need: it may be large or small; needed quickly, or without appreciable consideration of time. That, simply enough – in description at least – is the batsman's job. Within it he must be able to balance risks and hazards, and to weigh tactics.

In this position the ordinary batsman, when restricted and held back from his objective, will either accept the curb imposed by the bowler, or take the risk of knocking him off when more often than not the good bowler will defeat him. It has been the prerogative only of the great to destroy the best bowlers. Walter Hammond, for instance, finding his cover-driving checked by a slow left-arm bowler accurate enough to bowl to a packed off-side field and contain him, would go down on one knee and sweep, with a horizontal bat, to square-leg or finer, until the bowler was forced to transfer one or two fieldsmen from off to leg, when Hammond would take his runs through the off-side. On a number of occasions frequent enough for the Gloucestershire players to remember them ruefully, Jack Hobbs played Surrey out of trouble on the turning wickets which used so often to occur on the Cheltenham College ground. Charlie Parker was a master left-arm spinner who could make the ball talk on a responsive pitch. For Hobbs, the only method of preventing him wrecking the innings was to go down the pitch and hit him over extra cover, mid-off and mid-on until Charlie, in the words of one of his team-mates, 'couldn't and wouldn't bowl at him any more; and sulked off to third man'. Such methods, though, are for the great; and the more difficult against a skilful bowler and a captain who knows exactly what he is trying to do. The attacking batsman taking an observable risk and getting away with it is always relished by all but the most partisan spectators.

Batting which reaches perfection can seem almost ordinary, because everything seems so natural as to be unremarkable. The perceptive spectator will study the batsman at the opposite end, observe his difficulties, and appreciate the skill of 'ordinary perfection'.

The tactic of the counter punch is invariably stirring. Gilbert Jessop, for instance, used to counter-attack even against the finest bowling. Short, thick- and wide-shouldered, known as 'the Croucher' because of his low, belligerent stance, he had the orthodox strokes but he would also play unorthodoxly – especially the pull – in contradiction of the ball bowled. No other hitter ever had quite such success. He scored two fifties in a quarter of an hour; eleven centuries in an hour or less (including one in 40 minutes and one in 42); 150 in 63 minutes; four double hundreds in under an hour and a half. For England against Australia at The Oval in 1902, he scored his match-winning 104 in 75 minutes, off only 75 balls. No one else has ever scored quite so fast, so often, and so consistently. If three are to be chosen from among his many batting attributes, they must be his speed of footwork, eye and timing. Jessop, on his day was, in the words of one great bowler 'impossible to bowl to'.

In recent years, allowing for the fall in the over-rate since Jessop's day, such batsmen as Ian Botham, Clive Lloyd and Viv Richards have aroused similar responses.

Cricketers are as different as batsmen as they are as human beings: bold, cautious, aggressive, thoughtful, forceful, deflective, elegant, taut, anxious, rarely carefree. Batting, in all its moods, its varying tempos, and in its contrasting shades, and phases of character, can be beguiling or stimulating to watch; and it is constantly fresh, perpetually revealing new depths and facets of the men and their craft.

Chapter 11

UMPIRING

The umpires are established – there is a temptation to say 'enshrined' – in the *Laws of Cricket*. Law 3 stipulates that 'Before the toss for innings, two Umpires shall be appointed, one for each end, to control the game with absolute impartiality as required by the Laws.' (Raymond Robertson-Glasgow once humorously reminded an old umpire friend that the law said 'one for each end' and not 'one for each side'.) Although they stand one at each end, the new clause 10 specifies that 'The umpires shall stand where they can best see any act upon which their decision may be required. Subject to this over-riding consideration, the Umpire at the Bowler's end shall stand where he does not interfere with either the Bowler's run up or the Striker's view. The Umpire at the Striker's end may elect to stand on the off, instead of the leg, side of the pitch, provided he informs the Captain of the fielding and the Striker of his intention.' Clause 12 states 'All disputes shall be determined by the Umpires and if they disagree the actual state of things shall continue.'

The second and third clauses of the last Law – 42 – place the matter beyond question: 'The Umpires are the sole judges of fair and unfair play. The Umpires shall intervene without appeal by calling and signalling "dead ball" in the case of unfair play.'

Apart from a use of capital letters which recalls *The Pilgrim's Progress*, it could hardly be clearer; it tells us, them, and the players, exactly where they stand.

The office of Umpire – sorry, umpire – is an ancient one. It is also highly necessary; indeed, it is impossible to believe that a cricket match could be played without umpires. The earliest indication of the disciplines of the game occurs in the 'articles of agreement' for two matches to be played between teams raised by the Duke of Richmond and Mr Brodrick of Pepperharrow in 1727. Specific agreement on numerous points was necessary because the games – home and away – were to be played for a considerable wager. The articles are framed as 'instructions to umpires and team managers' and they elucidate possible grounds for dispute. The first full code of laws was framed in 1744; but it is significant that, long before, the conduct of the game was administered by umpires.

Some of older generations will recall umpires leaning on a bat or even a stick. That inherited from an extremely ancient tradition, as was made clear in the Richmond/Brodrick 'articles': 'The batsmen, for every run they count, are to touch the umpire's stick.'

The standing of umpires has varied over the ages. In the last century, Victorian humorists and comic artists tended to make game of them – largely, we may imagine, because Victorian sporting morality made their authority secure. In every age, though, there have been the acknowledged great umpires. In early days, there were Caldecourt, of whom contemporary prints bore the simple words 'The Umpire'; William Beagley, who was also a considerable batsman; Jim Phillips, of Victoria and Middlesex, who, between 1897 and 1901, in both England and Australia 'no balled' a series of unfair bowlers so effectively as to stamp out throwing for some fifty years.

Later, between the two wars, came the astute, if later eccentric, Frank Chester; a promising batsman with Worcestershire, whose playing career was ended by the loss of a hand in the war of 1914. Slightly his junior was Dai Davies; a shrewd, relishable character. Recently, the positive Charlie Elliott; the relaxed but firm John Langridge; the judicial Sid Buller; and the calm Frank Lee. Different as they were as people, all were outstanding; lifting their prestige and that of their fellows higher, probably, than at any other period. A seal was placed upon their standing by the formation, and official recognition of, The Association of Cricket Umpires, which registers, instructs, examines and certificates umpires.

The classic umpiring story, which has been credited variously to Frank Lee, Sid Buller and Charlie Elliott – and it could relate to any one of them, so let us trust posterity may allow them to share it – concerns a single decision. A bowler of some pace was operating; the batsman played back, very close to the line; there was a click; the entire fielding side went up in appeal. 'Not out' said the umpire, who was rewarded with looks ranging from disbelief to disgust. At the end of the over he beckoned the disgruntled bowler, led him down the pitch and pointed to a red mark where the ball had brushed the outside of the off stump. 'I heard the click, too', he said 'but I saw the bat did not touch the ball.' The bowler had the good grace to apologize.

The burdens upon umpires, as on those in all other departments of the game, have increased considerably in the past few years. The over-limit game has changed the situation here as well as elsewhere. In the 1975 World Cup Final at Lord's 'Dicky' Bird and Tom Spencer were 'on parade' to supervise preparations by nine in the morning and 'stood' in the match from the 11 a.m. start until the finish at 8.43 p.m.

Physically exhausting as that may have been it was relatively simple by comparison with the changing regulations they must administer. Not so long ago all first-class umpires administered a uniform kind of cricket within their own particular world. Now the 'first-class' umpire, before he sets out to work in the morning, must ask himself: 'Do we start at 10.30, 10.45, 11.00, or 11.30? Do we play to the rules for a five-day Test; a three-day fixture in the Championship or – different again – between a county and the touring side; or one of the three- or two-day matches played by the Universities; or a one-day match?' In which last case, 'Are the rules those of the NatWest Trophy, the Benson & Hedges Cup, the John Player League or the Prudential one-day internationals?' It would be a ludicrous situation if authority, and those involved, did not regard it all so seriously.

England's leading umpires of the present day are the somewhat eccentric, but quick-witted and dedicated, H. D. – 'Dickie' – Bird and the less demonstrative David Constant. The standard, though, is uniformly high, despite greater stresses than their predecessors ever knew.

Leading Australian umpires have been George Hele (who stood over a long period, including the 'Bodyline' series), George Borthwick, Lou Rowan, Colin Egar and T. F. Brooks (whose retirement after one Test of the 1978–79 series there emphasized his feelings about the stresses to which umpires were being subjected).

Of course stories have been told about umpires as about most sections of the cricketing community. It is well to notice, though, that the subjects of some of the funniest of them, Alec Skelding and Bill Reeves, were among the most capable in that office.

In recent years there have been many – far too many – instances of the kind of 'dissent' which, in military terms, would be described as 'dumb insolence'. The television slow-motion play-back, which demonstrates to viewers the 'error' made by an umpire at a single sighting at full speed, has tended to make some of their audience criticize umpires in a totally unfair way. When Test captains join the criticism, voicing their complaints about a decision which has gone against them, you may be certain that they are the kind of people who would gloat about such a 'mistake' made in their favour.

Umpires are essentially human, in some ways the most human of cricketers. Most of them in England have been former players, anxious, because of their feeling for it, to stay within the game they adopted, not merely as a living, but as a way of living. They have rarely wanted to disturb their former friendly relations with the men they played with and against in their 'active' days. That has meant that, in after-play meetings, drinks in the bar or dinner in the hotel, they add to the depth of lore and reminiscence which is part of the richness of, especially, the English county game. It may also be argued, though, that that has in many cases led to an altogether too tolerant attitude towards not only slackness, but malpractices. Certainly it has meant that throwers have been pardoned until their unfairness became inescapable. There can be no doubt, either, that many fast bowlers have practised intimidating, short-pitched bowling with relative impunity when, according to the Laws, they should have been checked.

This disciplinary slackness was sensed as long ago as the nineteen-sixties, and strictly regarded by Charlie Elliott and Sid Buller, who agreed that they would never – and the operative word is 'never' – again accept a drink, a meal, or even a lift in a car from a player on whom they might have to pass judgement. For Sid Buller, who had no motor car to travel between matches or home, this was a considerable deprivation. It is a measure of his quality as an umpire that he never flinched from it.

It was hard enough on an umpire when the – often uninformed – spectators, or the media, pitched into him and pilloried him for – real or imaginary – error. When the players join in, they are, whether they realize it or not, contributing towards a slide into anarchy, which might – perhaps – be possible in some walks of life; but which, if it were allowed to develop, would simply destroy cricket.

Hitherto the question of 'sledging' – attempting to put a player, usually a batsman, off his game by 'snide' remarks, abuse or sheer obscenity – has been left largely for captains to deal with. It now seems clear that it must fall within the province of umpires.

The time has been reached when strong steps must be taken about all this. The resignation of Tom Brooks at the start of a Test series was a warning – not taken seriously enough – that good umpires can reach the conclusion that it simply is not worth it for them. In other countries, of course, umpiring is not a seven-days-a-week job. In

England it is; but not a well-paid one. If umpires are to be competent, honest, and firm – and if, even more important, umpires are to be recruited – they must be given power; a position of dignity; and the kind of salary that indicates the respect in which authority holds them.

In any event, particularly if that official reinforcement is withheld, the ordinary spectator ought honestly to back the old adage that 'the umpire's decision is final' – because it is. All the gesturing, griping and bawling will not change a decision once it is given: an umpire may change his mind, but he will not be bullied into it. Let us accept these decisions rather than lapse into aggro; that does no good, and merely impairs – even destroys – the enjoyment which is the main purpose of cricket.

A code of signals exists which enables umpires to communicate decisions and the scores to the scorers. They are illustrated on page 72. Once Bill Reeves, returning to a familiar ground, was not told that the scorers had been moved to a new position. Throughout the morning session he directed his signals to the beer tent.

In March 1953, Tom Smith, an experienced club umpire, wrote to a number of his friends with the same interest to suggest a meeting. As a result they founded the Association of Cricket Umpires (ACU) which has spread all over the cricket world and, by 1981, had grown to a membership of over 4000, with 208 affiliated associations. The Association, which publishes the authoritative text book on the subject, and holds examinations, has done much to improve the efficiency of umpiring at club level. It was given the mark of official approval when MCC invited Tom Smith, for 25 years its general secretary, to join its Laws Committee; and made him an honorary life member.

To go back to bedrock, the Richmond/Brodrick agreement concluded 'If any of the Gamesters shall speak or give their opinion on any point of the game they shall be turned out and voided the match.' The administrators of today have good reason to ponder that unequivocal decision.

Chapter 12

SCORING

No department of cricket has made more radical advance than scoring. In the earliest form known it consisted of a scorer with a knife cutting notches on a stick and an extra deep one every fifth or tenth run. Now a computer calculates players' statistics in detail, which are instantly transmitted on the television screen.

One of the best – by human and artistic standards – of all cricket paintings is 'The Scorer' by Thomas Henwood. Executed in 1842, it is of William Davies of Lewes Priory, obviously a rich character, in his wide-brimmed straw hat and strong spectacles, with his book, pencil, ale bottles and glass.

Since the decision of a cricket match depends on the runs scored on either side, the matter of counting them is crucial. Although the scorer performs that task, the ultimate responsibility for its accuracy, formerly vested in the captains, has now been transferred to the umpires.

Every schoolboy with any interest in cricket is familiar with the standard, and the relatively simple, scorebook which shows runs scored, mode of dismissal of batsmen, bowling, and records each ball thus

and on to a final total and bowling analysis.

In relatively recent years, however, there have been considerable developments. They were originated, it seems certain, by William Ferguson – the legendary 'Fergy' – who was scorer and baggage man to 43 English, Australian, New Zealand and South African touring teams over a career from 1905 to 1957, and including 208 Test Matches. He was credited with never having lost a single item of baggage on all those tours. More historically important, though, he introduced scoring charts – showing the direction and value of all the strokes played by individual batsmen; and what is generally called line-by-line scoring.

His scoring charts often proved extremely revealing of a batsman's strengths and weaknesses: a number of Test captains used to study them and, often, base tactics on them.

Bill Ferguson's line-by-line scoring method was taken up by Arthur Wrigley who, in 1934, was engaged by the BBC to keep score for Howard Marshall, who was then their cricket commentator. He developed it further; so, in turn, did Roy Webber, Jack Price and Bill Frindall, all of whom kept score for sound radio commentary. The present method shows every ball bowled and provides a complete and detailed record of almost everything that takes place on the field of play. It has been demonstrated by Bill Frindall in the BBC's book *Armchair Cricket*; and in several volumes of Test series published with his complete scoring sheets.

The old style book is still sufficient for the basic purpose of deciding the result of a match. For the enthusiast, the statistician, and anyone who may need to refer to any specific occurrence and its time and outcome, the line-by-line method is of immense assistance. Scoring counts: and, in first-class cricket, it has most happily given employment, in their relative old age, to some worthy former county cricketers.

The Umpire's Signals

OUT

BOUNDARY SIX

BOUNDARY FOUR

BYE

DEAD BALL

LEG-BYE

NO BALL

ONE SHORT

WIDE

Chapter 13

GLOSSARY

The significance of some terms and names not explained in the text.

APPEAL   Law 27 says 'An appeal "How's That?" shall cover all ways of being out . . . The Umpires shall not give a Batsman out unless appealed to by the other side, which shall be done prior to the Bowler beginning his run-up or bowling action to deliver the next ball.' The umpire in question will reply 'out' or 'not out'. Of course, in practice, when the wicket is hit, or a palpable catch is made, no appeal is necessary; in some less obvious cases of a catch, to the wicketkeeper for instance, the 'walkers' will give themselves out – by walking. In the instance of lbw, and, often, run out or stumped, the batsman himself cannot know; and it is a case for an appeal if a member of the fielding side thinks he was out. An appeal is also accepted in such terms as 'How is *that*?', 'How *was* that?', 'Huzzat?', 'Haaaaat?' or even in extreme cases 'What about that then, ump?'

There is no official signal for 'not out'; but for 'out' *see* opposite.

ASHES   In every Test series between England and Australia 'the Ashes' are said to be at issue. This results from a mock obituary published in *The Sporting Times* on the day after England were beaten by Australia, not for the first time, but for the first time in England. The item read:

In affectionate remembrance
of
English Cricket
which died at the Oval, 28 August, 1882, deeply
lamented by a large circle of sorrowing friends and
acquaintances.
R.I.P.
N.B. The body will be cremated and the Ashes taken to
Australia.

In the following winter of 1882–83, the Hon. Ivo Bligh took an English team to Australia. After they had won two of the originally scheduled three Test Matches, two English ladies burnt a set of bails, put the ashes in an urn and presented it to the captain. The urn rests always at Lord's but, fictionally at least, passes with victory to either side or remains after an undecided rubber.

BACKING UP   May mean a non-striker advancing a stride or two down the pitch in anticipation of taking a quick run. Alternatively it means a fieldsman moving up, in support, behind another moving to field the ball; or behind the wicketkeeper or other fielder waiting at the stumps to collect a throw-in.

BEAMER   A fast, high, full pitch aimed at the head. Clause 9 of Law 42 declares it 'unfair'.

BENSON & HEDGES CUP   An over-limit competition which includes the seventeen first-class counties, Oxford and Cambridge Universities combined, Scotland, and a representative team chosen from all the Minor Counties. The innings are limited to 55 overs each and no bowler may bowl more than eleven overs in a match. The form of the competition is a combination of league and knock-out. The twenty competing teams are divided into four groups of five: each team plays each of the others in its group (two points for a win, one each for an unfinished match). In the event of two teams finishing their group with equal numbers of points, their positions are decided by striking rate: that is calculated on all group matches by dividing the number of overs bowled by the wickets taken (the faster – i.e. the lower average – takes precedence). The top two teams in each group go on to the quarter-finals of the conclusive knock-out competition, with a final at Lord's. The Benson & Hedges World Series Cup 1980–81 was competed for in a series of international over-limit matches organized by WSC in Australia.

BOUNCER or BUMPER   A fast, short-pitched ball.

BOUNDARY   The limit of the playing area of a cricket ground. It may be marked by a white line, rope, series of flags, board or fence. A ball crossing it after pitching counts four runs; without pitching, six. For the umpire's signals, *see* page 72.

BREAK BACK   A (sharp) off-break.

BUMP BALL   A colloquial term for a ball which, hit into the ground or trapped between bat and ground, pops up or flies and gives some the impression of being a catch.

BYE   When a ball – not wide or a no-ball – passes the striker without touching him or his bat, any runs the batsmen can run count as extras, and are entered under byes. As a general rule this means that the ball will also have passed the wicketkeeper. That is not always necessarily so, since at times – desperate times – batsmen may attempt to 'run to the wicketkeeper'. For the umpire's signal, *see* page 72.

CARRIES HIS BAT   When a man goes in first and is not out at the end of a complete innings.

COUNTY CHAMPIONSHIP   The major domestic competition of English cricket, called for the moment the Britannic Championship, and the only one in the world involving more or less daily play throughout the season. It forms, in some ways, the hub of world cricket. Economically, too, apart from some of the British leagues and isolated instances overseas, it is the only place in the world where a cricketer may find regular professional employment. Generally accepted as dating from 1873, it represents the body of the highly professional cricket in which its true and major skills have been developed. English cricket at the highest level could hardly exist – certainly not in any semblance of its present or traditional shape – without the Championship. Its form has been varied from time to time but its membership has now been unchanged for over sixty years. The seventeen English and Welsh first-class counties are those which compete in the Championship. The original nine (of 1873) were Derbyshire, Gloucestershire, Kent, Lancashire, Middlesex, Nottinghamshire, Surrey, Sussex and Yorkshire. At the end of 1887 Derbyshire withdrew; Somerset were brought in in 1891. In 1895, Derbyshire returned and Essex, Hampshire, Leicestershire, Warwickshire and Worcestershire came in; followed by Northamptonshire in 1905 and Glamorgan in 1921. Since the hunger for watching three-day play waned until it became uneconomic in about 1951, the Championship, of itself, has been far from financially self-supporting. Indeed, it probably was the most generous and valuable, because apparently the least worthy, of all the cricketing sponsorships when, in 1984, the Britannic Assurance decided to back it. The Championship is, in the eyes of county cricketers, above all others, the title to win; the sternest trial of strength and temperament. Its form – number of matches, basis of evaluation, method of scoring and of arranging fixtures – has varied constantly and widely. Since 1977, however, it has been based on a programme of each county playing twenty-two matches a season.

COVERING   So far as the laws are concerned, the pitch may be covered until a match begins; and the area of the bowlers' run-up at any time when it is considered desirable. In practice, covering is governed by playing regulations. So far as Tests, all first-class matches and the three county one-day competitions are concerned, that means the pitch is covered before the match and, once it has started, against any rain sufficient to stop play, or which falls outside playing hours. That virtually eliminates the element of weather-chance which in the past made English cricket so absorbingly unpredictable and created the 'sticky' wickets which showed off great spin bowlers and batsmen to the highest advantage. Covers vary widely in their degree of effectiveness; although they have been vastly improved in the past decade, none has yet been found perfect.

CRICKETERS' ASSOCIATION Founded in 1968 by Fred Rumsey, the Worcestershire and Somerset fast bowler. It is the association of active county cricketers in England; usually regarded as their trade union, though they say it is not. The Secretary is J. D. Bannister, formerly of Warwickshire; the Chairman, Chris Balderstone of Leicestershire. It negotiates players' conditions and minimum wages, and often acts on their behalf in professional matters.

CRICKET COUNCIL, THE   The ruling body responsible for the broad areas of activity of the game in England, it is composed of: the National Cricket Association, whose function is to coordinate and foster all aspects of the game short of first-class, notably coaching; the Test and County Cricket Board (TCCB), responsible for the first-class game; and the MCC, which provides headquarters and the administrative centre.

DANGER AREA   An area two feet wide running for one foot on either side of the line from one middle stump to the other, and beginning four feet in front of the stumps, has been designated a 'danger area'. That means that umpires are required to protect it from damage – even though accidental – by batsmen running down the wicket, bowlers following through, or fieldsmen crossing. A bowler persistently offending is to be cautioned, and, if he continues to offend, given a final warning, and then, if he still persists, his captain must be ordered to take him off for the rest of the innings. He will then be reported to the TCCB.

DEAD BALL   Once the ball is 'dead', no wicket can be taken and no run scored. The reasons for a ball being dead number fifteen, all of which are fairly obvious; the most notable is when the umpire intervenes in a case of unfair play. Those who wish to examine them further will find them listed in clauses 1 and 2 of Law 23; six occasions when it might be considered, but is not, are included in clauses 3 and 4 of the same law. The umpire both calls and signals 'dead ball' – *see* page 72.

DECLARATION A captain may declare his side's innings closed (i.e. end it) regardless of the number of wickets down – at any time he wishes. In practice that generally happens, in a first innings, when he feels they probably have scored enough for his ultimate purpose of winning the match. In the second innings the situation may be the same; on the other hand he may feel that his only reasonable hope of winning is to declare, even though that means giving the other side a chance to win also. Surprisingly enough this latter course, now quite common, is a relatively new tactic in the county game. Until the 1950s, sides used often to bat on to a draw rather than gamble defeat against a win. A captain may also forfeit an innings; this would generally happen only where much time had been lost to rain and he wished to go for a finish at all costs.

DONKEY DROP A high, slow, full toss designed – hopefully – to fall on top of the stumps.

DRAW An unfinished match; or a stroke – characteristic of mid-nineteenth-century batsmen – in which the front foot was raised high and the ball glanced between the legs.

DRINKS A prospect of immense and attractive scope and variations. In this context, though, it refers to the liquid refreshment which officially may be taken out to any team once in each session of play. The operative word is 'may'. The fielding captain can decide not to take the drinks except in trying climatic conditions. The drinking habits of great – and less than great – cricketers make an absorbing topic; but this is not the place to enlarge upon it.

EXTRAS Runs added to a team's score which are not made by the batsman but represent penalties of various types imposed on the fielding side. They consist of no-balls, byes, leg-byes and wides (q.v.).

FIRST-CLASS A first-class match is one so designated by the cricketing authority of the country in which it is played; but it must be between two teams of eleven players each, and must last for at least three days. The local authority decides whether the players are of a quality for their cricket to be described as first-class. For first-class counties, *see* County Championship.

FITNESS   Not in this a matter of physical condition but of the fitness or otherwise of conditions for play. Clause 8 of Law 3 places upon the umpires the responsibility for deciding whether the pitch, light and weather are such that it would be proper to play. Even, however, if they decide that the conditions are not fit, the players may – at the wish of both captains – continue to play (i.e. through rain or in bad light).

FLIGHT   The ability of some (slow) bowlers to deceive a batsman as to the length of the ball by dip or apparent check through the air.

FLY SLIP   A fielding position only occasionally used; mid-way between slips and third man, intended to catch out a slashing or slicing batsman.

FOLLOW ON   If a side is 200 runs behind in a five-day match; 150 in a three- or four-day; 100 in a two-day, or 75 in a one-day, the opposing captain may invite – splendid word – them to 'follow their innings', i.e. bat again immediately. In that event he can reserve his second innings.

FULL TOSS   Or full pitch; a ball which reaches the batsman without having bounced.

GILLETTE CUP   No longer exists. It was the first of the English county over-limit competitions. It began in 1963. When the Gillette sponsorship ceased in 1980 it passed to the National Westminster Bank and became the NatWest Bank Trophy (q.v.).

GOING AWAY   A ball that leaves the bat.

GUARD   The batsman may request, and the umpire will indicate to him – usually from over the stumps, unless he requests another line (perhaps from the bowler's point of delivery) – generally the line to his middle, middle-and-leg, or leg stump. There he may make his mark (or block hole) and that is where he will ground his bat when he takes his stance, knowing his position in relation to his stumps.

HALF-VOLLEY   A ball which may be hit in the moment after it pitches. Except on an atrocious pitch it offers runs, and should be hit.

HAT TRICK   The feat by a bowler of taking three wickets with consecutive balls. They need not be in the same over – they may be in consecutive overs; or carry over from the end of one innings to the beginning of the next – but must be in the same match. The term derives from the former custom of presenting the bowler responsible with a (top) hat.

ICC/INTERNATIONAL CRICKET CONFERENCE Formerly the Imperial Cricket Conference, founded 1909. Full Members: England, Australia, West Indies, India, New Zealand, Pakistan, Sri Lanka. Associate Members: Holland, Denmark, Canada, Argentina, Gibraltar, Israel, Malaysia, Hong Kong, Papua New Guinea, Bermuda, USA, East Africa, Singapore, Fiji. The international body of cricket dominated, of course, by the full members. Generally meets during the Lord's Test Match of every season; but its major meeting is for the four-yearly World Cup when virtually all the member countries compete.

INFIELD The close and the partway fieldsmen, as distinct from the outfield.

INSLANT Bowling, usually directed from the edge of the crease, by a right-arm over-the-wicket bowler and directed at, or even outside, the leg-stump. The ultimately negative form of bowling.

INTIMIDATION Clause 8 of Law 42 places yet another decision on the shoulders of the umpires. That is the decision as to whether the bowling of 'fast short-pitched balls' (in general parlance, bouncers, or bumpers) is an attempt to intimidate the batsman. If so, he will first caution the bowler; on repetition administer a final warning, and if it is repeated, have the bowler taken off for the remainder of the innings and report the matter to the offender's national authority.

JOHN PLAYER LEAGUE The Sunday League; the competition created by the English cricketing authority in reaction to the attraction – to spectators but especially to television – of the Rothmans Cavaliers. It began in 1969 and consists of 40-over matches between the seventeen first-class counties who play each other once during the season. Scoring is four points for a win; two for a tie or no result. If, at the end of the competition, teams are equal on points, precedence goes to the one with the most wins; if that produces no result, the one with most away wins; the final resort is the best scoring rate (runs divided by overs) over the entire season.

LAP Dressing-room slang for the cross-batted stroke which 'carts' the ball roughly towards square-leg.

LEG BEFORE WICKET (LBW) The leg-before law is discussed on page 8. Yet it cannot be overstressed that this is the decision on which there is most, and most frequent, dissent. It is all too easy – especially for the beginner umpire – to give a decision based on the spontaneous reaction 'Oh, that would have hit'. That, though, is not the sole criterion. The good umpire will ask himself: Where did the ball pitch? Where did the pad stop it? Would it have passed the stumps on either side? Might it have passed over the stumps? and, in the off-side proviso, Was the batsman trying to play it? All these points must be weighed. Dai Davies, wise old umpire, pondered his lbw decisions so long that he called his 'Out' for lbw 'the slow death'.

LEG BYE An 'extra', or extras, scored when the ball runs off the batsman's dress or body – but not the bat, nor the hand holding it – and the batsmen are able to take runs before it is retrieved and returned. The essential point about leg byes is that the contact with the body or dress must be unintentional on the batsman's part. For the umpire's signal, *see* page 72.

LEG CUTTER In effect a leg-break, it turns from leg towards off; but it is produced by the drag down from the inswinger's grip and not by the normal leg-break spin.

LEG THEORY When Fred Root bowled his sharp, late inswing – varied with one which went the other way – to a novel close leg-side field, and batsmen counter-attacked, hitting over or through his field, his – attacking – leg theory could seem exciting. With the increasing efficiency and placing of short-leg fieldsmen, the restrictive purpose, not simply of inswing, but of inslant, it has become a negative tactic, making for low- and slow-scoring dullness.

LEG TRAP The ring of close leg-side fieldsmen set by off-spinners, inswingers, inslanters and the purveyors of fast short-pitched bowling at the head, in the hope that from all the varying strategies of such varied bowling, they will make a catch.

LONG FIELD Boundary field, and fieldsmen.

LONG HOP An evocative description for a very short-pitched ball; in effect a free hit (hook or square cut).

MAIDEN OVER An over off which no run is scored from the bat. If a wicket falls in the course of it, it is called a 'wicket maiden'.

MCC/MARYLEBONE CRICKET CLUB A private club formed in 1787,

which is the accepted law-making body of the game. It owns Lord's Cricket Ground, London, NW8, where it houses the administration of the ICC, the Cricket Council, TCCB, NCA and the Middlesex County Cricket Club.

MATTING   A form of artificial strip wicket, made usually of hemp or similar material, used where good turf pitches cannot be laid. For many years first-class cricket was played in South Africa, and subsequently in Pakistan, on such pitches. They produced some extremely fine specialist spinners of pace between slow and medium, such as the South African wrist-spinners, and the faster E. P. 'Buster' Nupen and Fazal Mahmood.

MINOR COUNTIES   The English and Welsh domestic competition which from time to time includes the Second XIs of first-class counties. Currently there are 19 Minor County entrants. They also raise a representative team, often to play the touring side, and also to enter the Benson & Hedges Cup.

NCA/NATIONAL CRICKET ASSOCIATION   Originally set up in 1965 as the MCC Cricket Association. Its duty is to coordinate and foster all aspects of the game short of first-class, notably coaching, at all levels, on a national basis.

NATWEST BANK TROPHY   An over-limit competition inheriting from the Gillette Cup, which it replaced in 1981. It is purely a knock-out competition, played between the seventeen first-class counties and the top five from the Minor Counties Championship of the previous season. It is in most ways the fullest of the one-day competitions; the innings are of a maximum of sixty overs; of which no one bowler may deliver more than twelve.

NEW BALL   Generally considered to swing more, and bounce in livelier fashion, than a more worn ball: and therefore more desirable to the faster and swing bowlers. Its availability has been the subject of discussion and changing legislation for many years. It is now given to the governing bodies of the game in different countries to decide when it shall be available, with a recommended minimum of 75 overs.

NIGHT WATCHMAN   Dressing-room term for the – usually – late-order batsman sent in towards the end of the day in the hope of protecting the wicket of a better batsman until the morning.

NO-BALL   An illegal delivery, so adjudged, called and signalled by the umpire; whereupon one run – recorded as an extra – is awarded to the batting side. If, however, the batsman strikes it, he and his partner may run as many runs as they can, as if it had been a legal delivery. A batsman may be run out from a no-ball; but not bowled, caught or stumped. There are various minor technicalities concerning a no-ball. Usually, the umpire decides it is illegal because the bowler either did not have some part of the front foot – in the air or on the ground – behind the popping crease; or his back foot within – not touching – the line of the return crease (*see* page 4). Most important, and more rarely, a bowler may be called for an unfair delivery because he was adjudged to have thrown the ball – i.e. to have bent or, more usually, straightened his arm in the process of delivery. For the umpire's signal, *see* page 72.

NON-STRIKER   The batsman who is not receiving the bowling.

OFF-CUTTER   In effect an off-break, but produced by dragging the fingers down the seam from swinger's grip as distinct from the normal finger-spin method.

OUTCRICKET   The operations of the fielding side, bowling, wicket-keeping and fielding.

OUTFIELD   The deep fieldsmen guarding the boundaries.

OVER   The number of balls to be delivered by a bowler before the bowling switches to the other end. The earliest known 'over' consisted of four balls; in 1889 it was increased to five; in 1900 to six. In 1918 Australia adopted the eight-ball over; New Zealand experimented with eight from 1924 to 1926; England in 1939; South Africa from 1937 to 1939; West Indies in 1946–47. Australia reverted to six-ball for 1979–80.

In 1946 D. F. Hill, bowling for British Guiana against Barbados, bowled an 'over' of 14 balls. There were no wides or no balls; but the umpire miscounted the 'eight-ball' over. The fourteenth ball bowled out Everton Weekes.

OVER THE WICKET   Bowling with the operative bowling arm nearer to the stumps (*see* Round the wicket).

OVERTHROWS   Runs accruing from a return which eludes the wicket-keeper or other fieldsman guarding the stumps. If a throw hits the stumps – with the batsman in his ground – and ricochets away, runs may be taken.

PAIR   Short for a 'pair of spectacles', the sad experience for a batsman of a 'duck' (nought) in each innings. A 'king pair' is a nought from the first ball received in each innings.

PLAYED ON   The ball runs into the stumps and breaks the wicket after being in contact with the bat. It is entered in the score book as 'bowled'.

PRUDENTIAL   The insurance company which has sponsored, subsidized and given its name to the 'World Cup' of one-day cricket; and also to the one-day internationals which preceded Test series in England. It withdraws from cricket after the 1983 World Cup.

QUALIFICATION (for country or county)   *See* Registration.

REGISTRATION AND QUALIFICATION   The two are not the same. A cricketer needs to be qualified to play for a country; he must be both qualified and registered to play for a county. The question of whether or not a cricketer might play for a country or county used to be – or seemed to be – relatively simple. Occasionally, as in the case of Lord Harris's protest against Wally Hammond playing for Gloucestershire, it could produce bitterness; and it was often inconvenient, even uncomfortable, for young cricketers qualifying by residence in indifferent lodgings. Yet it all seemed fairly straightforward; now it is not.

Every country makes its own regulations about who may play for it or in its domestic competitions; and, since they may differ, these notes refer to England only. They are complex. Thus, county birth or residential qualification is decided by recourse to 'the boundaries shown in red as administrative county boundaries on Ordnance Survey 1/625000 as at 1st April 1972; save the County of London which shall be deemed divided as it was prior to 1st April 1965.' In such a legalistic atmosphere, precise explanation would occupy a disproportionate amount of this book: and the situation remains matter for debate. Basic principles, though, are as follows for the time being.

A cricketer may play for England (1) if he was born there, or (2) his mother or father was born there; *and* he has lived there for four years; and, in both cases, if he has not played for another country in the previous four years. (3) If he has lived in England and not played for any other country during the previous ten years. (4) If he has lived in England during the previous four years *and* since the day before his fourteenth birthday; *and* has not played for any other country during any of those periods.

In the last three cases he must also be a British or Irish citizen; in all he must declare in writing that he wants to play for England if selected.

By comparison, the matter of county registration is more complex and should be reduced to two main sections. In the first case, of English or English-resident cricketers with no existing ties with other countries. A cricketer *qualified to play for England* may play for the county of his birth; the county in which he has lived for the previous year; the county for which his father played regularly; or if he is not registered – or wanted to be registered – for another entitled county.

Special registration does not now mean what it used to mean. A cricketer *qualified to play for England* may be specially registered for a county if the TCCB decides that it would be in the best interests of county cricket. All those points are subject to qualification, discussion and judgement by the TCCB.

Now to the matter of 'unqualified cricketers' – who used to be described as 'overseas stars' or 'special registrations'. They are *not* qualified to play for England. They are cricketers who play, or have lately played, in or for other countries; but whom English counties would like to engage in order to strengthen their sides. The engagement of overseas cricketers was allowed to run almost wild from 1968 until 1979 when, all at once, the TCCB clamped down. Without exhuming too many qualifications, the basic ruling is that a county may only play *one* such 'unqualified player' in any competitive county match. There is, though, a proviso, framed to avoid employment hardships to players, which permits a county to play *two* provided *both* were signed before the start of the 1979 season; or any two who regularly played in 1974 and 1975.

The ramifications and safeguards about 'poaching' players, negotiations, registrations and cancellations are infinite. They are usually explained in the press when a dispute arises.

RETIREMENT A batsman may retire from the crease at any time; but, unless he does so for injury or illness, he may not return.

ROLLING, MOWING AND WATERING The pitch may be rolled – and swept – for seven minutes before the start of each day's play; and before the start of each innings. It may be mowed – under the supervision of the umpires – before the start of play on alternate days. Since Sunday counts, in a Test in England it may be mowed on Thursday, Saturday and Monday. The pitch may not, under any circumstances, be watered at any time after play has begun.

ROUND THE WICKET   A bowler delivering with his bowling arm further from the stumps.

RUNNER   A man running between wickets for a batsman unable to run for himself.

SHOOTER   A ball which, instead of bouncing, shoots along the ground; a freak; so far as batsmen are concerned, a horror.

SHORT RUN   Where a batsman does not make good his ground before turning for another run. The run is disallowed and the umpire will call, and signal 'one short' – *see* page 72.

SIGHT SCREEN   The white – or sometimes pale blue or green – boarding placed behind the bowler's arm to afford the batsman a background for a clear sight of the ball.

SINGLE WICKET   A form of cricketing single combat practised, especially, up to the middle of the nineteenth century; largely as a public spectacle. The rules of play varied enormously but in its most usual form, two cricketers competed against each other, batting and bowling in turn. When each bowled he had the support of – as a rule – five fieldsmen. Runs could not be scored behind the wicket. It was revived, under sponsorship, in England between 1963 and 1969; when the final of the competition was held at Lord's. It proved mildly entertaining but not truly convincing.

STRIKER   The term of the Laws for the batsman receiving the bowling.

SUBSTITUTE   A stand-in – as fieldsman or runner only – for an injured or otherwise incapacitated player. He may, however, only act in this capacity with the approval of the opposing captain.

SWEEP   A stroke – of which Denis Compton was the ultimate master – which does, in fact, sweep the ball – especially an off-break – from on or outside the leg stump (sometimes, in the case of DCS, nearer middle) to leg, generally fine of square.

TAIL   The lower order batting.

TCCB/TEST AND COUNTY CRICKET BOARD   The authority responsible for the administration of Test and county cricket in and for England. Its office is at Lord's: Secretary, D. B. Carr.

TEST MATCH   An international cricket match played between two full members of the International Cricket Conference. They are England, Australia, West Indies, India, New Zealand, Pakistan and Sri Lanka.

THROW   The fieldsman's return to the wicket; but see 'No-ball'.

TIME WASTING   It is unfair to waste time. When it is done it is usually for a tactical reason to prevent the other side from exploiting a winning position. The umpires are required to warn any player responsible – batsman, fielder or bowler – and to register the fact with his captain. The matter should also be reported to the authority with jurisdiction over the player.

TOSS   Before the start of a cricket match, the captains of the opposing sides meet; one – usually the captain of the home side – tosses a coin; and the other calls. The winner of the toss has the choice of taking first innings for his team, or inviting the opponents to bat.

TWELFTH MAN   The 'extra' or reserve player who will usually act as substitute if one is required. More often he finds himself the team's general dogsbody; mainly drinks waiter.

WICKET MAIDEN   A maiden over – i.e. one from which no runs are scored – but in which a wicket(s) falls.

WIDE   A ball bowled so high or wide of the batsman that, in the umpire's opinion, he cannot hit it. A wide counts one run; but, if it passes the wicketkeeper, the batsmen may run as in the case of byes. If it goes to the boundary it counts 'four wides'. For the umpire's signal, *see* page 72.

WISDEN TROPHY   The trophy awarded for Test series between England and the West Indies.

WISDEN   *Wisden Cricketers' Almanack*, first published by the Sussex cricketer, John Wisden, in 1864, is the recognized annual record of the game.

WRONG 'UN   A slang term for the googly.

YORKER   A bowler may 'york' a batsman, but he cannot positively bowl a yorker. The batsman creates a yorker, by playing a full toss as a half volley; or a half volley as a full toss: it passes under his bat.

Chapter 14

THE COUNTIES

The major historic change in the shape of English county cricket since the Second World War has been the levelling up (though some might call it a levelling down) of achievement among the counties. Even in the Edwardian so-called Golden Age – 1900 to 1914 – the Championship was almost grotesquely uneven. Yorkshire, Middlesex, Lancashire, Kent, Nottinghamshire and Surrey dominated it; only Warwickshire, in 1911, interrupted their monopoly of the title. Meanwhile, Essex, Leicestershire, Gloucestershire, Somerset and Derbyshire rarely, if ever, attained a single-figure position in the table. Even in the inter-war period when Yorkshire were twelve times Champions, and Lancashire five, Glamorgan, Northamptonshire, Worcestershire, Hampshire and Somerset were regular chopping-blocks. Indeed, Northamptonshire never, and Worcestershire only once, finished higher than eleventh, while Glamorgan and Leicestershire were only twice higher than tenth. That situation, thanks, in part, to the one-day competitions, no longer exists.

In the post-1945 period, though, Glamorgan, Hampshire, Worcestershire, Leicestershire and Essex have all won the Championship for the first time; while three counties who have never held that title, Somerset – regularly now one of the strongest teams in the country – Sussex and Northamptonshire, have all won the Gillette (or NatWest) trophy. So, too, have Gloucestershire who had not won the Championship since 1877. Even so, Yorkshire won eight outright Championships and shared one; while Surrey were winners seven years in succession, 1952 to 1958.

The permitted registration of overseas players undoubtedly lifted the standards of English county cricket; and many young English players profited from the influence of the newcomers. They undoubtedly provided crucial strengthening to some counties, several of which must find themselves substantially weakened by any limitation imposed on them. The following notes may provide some indication of the strengths, weaknesses and interesting aspects of the individual counties. Much, though, will depend on the course that legislation on the use of overseas players may take.

DERBYSHIRE

When, in 1983, Derbyshire made Kim Barnett, twenty-two years old, the youngest captain in their history, they took an apparent risk which, in the event, changed the character of their team for the better. Barnett himself made a considerable advance as a batsman and, handicapped as he was by the absence of, and injury to, his most experienced players, he led the county to one of their most successful seasons for some twenty years.

So, much now lies open to a purposeful and contented team. If, after the West Indian tour of 1984, they should have the fast bowler, Michael Holding, regularly available, and Paul Newman fully fit, they would have an extremely hostile opening pair. Those two could link with Ole Mortensen, the Danish seam bowler, plus the spinners Dallas Moir – who had the usual setback season in 1983 – and a fit Geoff Miller, to form a well-balanced bowling side. The problems of 1983 drew encouraging responses from the young Roger Finney, Bill Fowler and John Morris. Derbyshire have, too, reached an arrangement with Leslayne Lambert, a fast bowler from Guyana, in case Holding should be unavailable in 1984.

Enjoy: Barnett's leg-spin – when he puts himself on – and John Hampshire's inherently joyous batting.

ESSEX

A side with a relatively small staff, but, nevertheless, of strength in depth. Essex showed great resolve in coming from behind Middlesex to win the Championship in 1983. They had the advantage, of course, of losing only one player to Test calls since others who might have been chosen were under Test suspension for their South African escapade: but it was a highly capable performance.

Keith Fletcher is a shrewd captain who has the wholehearted backing of his side; and he remains one of the finest players of spin bowling in the world.

Essex bat long and entertainingly; Graham Gooch and Chris Gladwin are as enterprising an opening pair as any in the country. It had been said that the side which won the Championship in 1979 were all ageing together. Then David East (the wicketkeeper), Derek Pringle, Chris Gladwin and the exciting prospect, Neil Foster, all suddenly 'showed' to make the team look young again.

In addition Alan Lilley, who has produced some impressive performances in relatively few appearances, and the young England cap, Bob Leiper, are promising back-up players. Essex are happy not merely in their all-rounders; but also in batsmen who can bowl, and in bowlers – and a wicketkeeper – who can bat, and have often done so importantly at moments of need. They will be looking for a left-arm spinner to succeed Ray East; but much of their strength stems from anticipation of problems. The inability of as useful a cricketer as Keith Pont to command a regular team place is indicative of their resources.

Enjoy: the aggressive stroke-play of Graham Gooch; the subtle – and not easily observed – artifices of the philosophic off-spinner David Acfield.

GLAMORGAN

The retirement of Alan Jones, the opening batsman who scored over 35,000 runs for them, and that fine and thoughtful seam bowler, Malcolm Nash, at the end of 1983, marked the end of a period for Glamorgan. In a way, the recruitment of Mike Selvey and his appointment as captain in that year had already signalled the beginning of a new phase.

They have struggled with the problem of being able to play only one of their overseas players, the West Indian fast bowler, Winston Davis, or Javed Miandad, the brilliant Pakistani batsman; and have found this difficult to resolve.

Their fragile batting ought to be considerably strengthened by the addition of Younis Ahmed, whose ability is not to be doubted, and that industrious all-rounder, John Steele. They will be looking anxiously for the development as a batsman of the unmistakably talented Alan Lewis Jones; and to Charles Rowe – off-spinner and batsman – finding his feet. Barry Lloyd slipped back as an off-spinner; and Rodney Ontong worked hard to switch from seam to spin. David Francis, Mike Llewellyn and John Hopkins join a long list of the county's promising young players who still have not fully realized their potential. Mike Selvey's intelligent and enterprising captaincy ought to bring out the best in them. The long-term aim is to produce not merely a winning side but a winning side of Welsh-born players.

The county nurses high hopes of the batting potential of Stephen Henderson, the Cambridge captain; and even more of the Cardiff-born Hugh Morris, one of the most exciting young prospects in the country.

Enjoy: Javed Miandad's stroke-play – he is a world-class batsman – his cover-fielding and, when permitted, his buzzing leg-spin.

GLOUCESTERSHIRE

The retirement of Mike Procter left Gloucestershire in dire need of a strike bowler. Their batting is strong as any; in 1983 six men made a thousand runs, while Zaheer Abbas, able to play in only twelve matches, scored 867 at an average of 45. They also were torn between their two overseas players: Zaheer, one of the finest batsmen in the world, and Franklyn Stephenson, the Barbadian fast bowler.

John Shepherd, in his fortieth year, turned in a fine all-round performance; his medium-paced bowling gave him more wickets than anyone else; he constantly batted valuably; and held his catches. He could not, though, provide the cutting edge his captain, David Graveney, needed. Graveney probably under-bowled himself; but John Childs and Philip Bainbridge did not play to form. The main urgent hope is that David Lawrence, the young locally born pace bowler, will redeem his early promise.

Presumably greater batting ability has given 'Jack' Russell, a gritty cricketer, the position of wicketkeeper; which leaves one of the country's most talented players in that position in the country, Andy Brassington, in the second eleven. Surely some county must recruit so valuable a cricketer. Ironically enough, Andy Stovold, the lively opening batsman, can keep wicket capably enough in over-limit matches.

The advance of Paul Romaines has won him a county cap; and represents the grounding of a fresh generation.

The decision of Chris Broad to leave the county for better hopes of Test selection may seem a little arrogant; in his place, though, comes a highly gifted batsman, and useful change bowler, in Bill Athey from Yorkshire.

The Bristol pitch where, in their time, such spinners as Charlie Parker, Tom Goddard, Reg Sinfield, David Allen, John Mortimore and Sam Cook, flourished is no longer so helpful to spin as it was in their day; which represents a poor prospect for David Graveney and John Childs.

Enjoy: the splendidly relaxed stroke-play of Zaheer Abbas.

HAMPSHIRE

Hampshire enjoy considerable support from overseas players – speaking both cricketo-legally and actually. Their two West Indians, Malcolm Marshall – as fast as almost anyone in the present-day game – and the brilliantly explosive opening batsman, Gordon Greenidge, are registered as overseas players. The two Smith brothers come from South Africa but Christopher 'Kippy' – the elder – is qualified and, of course, has already played for England; while Robin also will be qualified in 1985 unless the rules are changed.

The solid batting of Trevor Jesty is further reinforced by the advance of Mark Nicholas and Paul Terry.

The bowling suffered from lack of spin and also by the loss of form of Kevin Emery who had been a major English batting discovery of 1982. Some compensation lay in the advance of Tim Tremlett, who increased his pace with notable effect. John Southern, the slow left-arm bowler, left the staff at the end of 1983; Rajesh Maru, a Kenyan off-spinner from the Lord's staff, was signed in his place, and Nick Taylor, fast medium from Yorkshire, has been recruited. Without their two West Indians, Hampshire would hardly hope to cut any great figure but they have Milton Small in reserve for Marshall; and there is much talent on the staff. Notably, Bobby Parks improves steadily as a wicketkeeper, and Nick Pocock is growing in stature as a captain.

Enjoy: Trevor Jesty's stylish batting; Gordon Greenidge's close-to-the-wicket fielding and immensely powerful strokes.

KENT

All through the 1970s Kent could be regarded as serious competitors for all the competitions; and an attractive side to watch. Into the eighties, perhaps because the team was partly in flux, they seemed to lose some of their earlier flair.

The talent, though, is there for them to return to the top. There is much batting talent, with Bob Woolmer's experience and Chris Tavare's solid determination as foundation. On that basis, Chris Cowdrey's splendid aggression, the youthful promise of Mark Benson – surely an England player of the future – and the budding talent of Derek Aslett can all flourish. There must be some disappointment that the gifted Laurie Potter has had so few opportunities and, perhaps, like a number of other promising Kent players of recent years, he should look for another county.

The bowling is still the main doubt about another series of major successes. Derek Underwood remains a splendid bowler for all settings and ocasions. Unfortunately, though, neither Kevin Jarvis nor Graham Dilley has been able consistently to produce the fast bowling form each displays sporadically. This, though, has enabled the persevering Richard Ellison and the West Indian, Eldine Baptiste, to seize their opportunities.

Alan Knott remains one of the world's two or three best wicket-keepers and a highly serviceable batsman. Indeed, the Kent staff must be counted fifteen strong of men who would not be out of place in the first team.

Enjoy: Derek Underwood's philosophic skills and patience; Chris Cowdrey's expansive batting; Alan Knott's acrobatic ability.

LANCASHIRE

It is difficult for anyone with a sense of the perspective of cricket history to write with satisfaction about Lancashire cricket of the post-war period. It is true that they were among the earliest to comprehend, and meet, the demands of the one-day game. Indeed, between 1969 and 1976 they six times reached the final of the Gillette Cup and four times won it; and were twice John Player League Champions. On the other hand, it is historically sad that one of the original 'big six' has not won the County Championship since 1934.

Most of the players of the one-day successes have left or are on the verge of retirement. By 1984 David Hughes and Clive Lloyd, two of the brightest stars of that fine phase, were talking clearly of finishing; while even the irrepressible Jack Simmons, despite a magnificent revival which averted so many crises for the side in

1983, was already forty-two. Frank Hayes had suffered from injuries; Andrew Kennedy, who held such high promise, had gone; and David Lloyd had departed to the league game.

So to the younger players: Ian Folley and Gary Speak, local products, of whom much was hoped in the desperately weak seam bowling sector, faded sadly in 1983 but remained young enough to come back; Watkinson, of lower pace, achieved more. The absence of Clive Lloyd allowed the inclusion of the South African Steve Jeffries, lively left-arm, who had one or two useful days. Too much depended on Paul Allott, who fell away after the World Cup.

Among the batsmen, Graham Fowler continued in his impressive advance; Steve O'Shaughnessy achieved an all too easy record fast century, but ought to bat lower than Lancashire use him. Their batting discovery of the season was Neil (Harvey) Fairbrother, a sturdy left-hander from Warrington.

In the absence of Clive Lloyd, John Abrahams proved an alert deputy captain, and simultaneously, and unusually, improved his batting. Nasir Zaidi bowled his leg-breaks and googlies artfully; batted boldly and fielded well; he deserves nursing. Lancashire, though, have much to do and far to go.

Enjoy: The fielding of Clive Lloyd; the stroke-play of Fowler; the panache in all departments of Nasir Zaidi; the imperishable zest of Jack Simmons.

LEICESTERSHIRE

After a remarkably brief period of team-rebuilding, Leicestershire were, by the middle of the 1980s, poised for further success. Once more the side had a balanced look. The bowling, with the high pace of young Antiguan George Ferris, the splendidly revived medium-paced skills of Paddy Clift, the supporting pace of Les Taylor, the slow spin of Nick Cook – a Test-class bowler – gave them a most excellent attack. Meanwhile they retain high hopes of Jonathan Agnew and Gordon Parsons. The handsome batting of David Gower is supported by the solidity of Chris Balderstone, the enterprise of Ian Butcher and the steady development of Nigel Briers. Mike Garnham had been brought along to replace Roger Tolchard. The important addition to the staff, however, was Peter Willey, almost of Test class as a batsman and, at a pinch, a useful off-spinner.

Much credit for foresight, team-building and perception of talent must go to Mike Turner, virtually the first of the secretary-manager-planners, who has been at the back of Leicestershire's progress for many seasons. He must be given his due, too, for the consistent reliance on Paddy Clift who, after injury and some worries, emerged in 1983 as the genuine all-rounder he had always promised to be.

Enjoy: the elegant stroke-play of David Gower; the old-fashioned merits of Nick Cook's slow left-arm; the immense variety of Paddy Clift's bowling; the high pace of George Ferris.

MIDDLESEX

For a decade from the mid-1970s, Middlesex were in serious contention for all the competitions, but especially for the County Championship. Apart from a surprising lapse in 1979, they were four times (once shared) Champions, once runners-up, once third, and once fourth. There may have been doubts as to how they might fare after the retirement of Mike Brearley; but they were soon dispelled. Mike Gatting succeeded him with no hint of the loss of playing form so many cricketers have evinced in their first seasons as county captains; and he was top of their batting averages.

It might be argued that they were unfortunate to lose the title in 1983 but, even at that time, they showed signs of increasing strength. Eleven batsmen averaged over 20 runs an innings; and, in the frequent absence of Norman Cowans, five other bowlers took 33 or more wickets at less than 26. Their attacking balance was enviable; Wayne Daniel, Neil Williams, Simon Hughes and, when available, Norman Cowans provided a sharp edge of pace. Most impressively, though, in not always helpful conditions, John Emburey and Philippe Edmonds took 168 wickets with their contrasting spins. Roland Butcher's advance as a batsman was halted by a savage injury; but Graham Barlow, promoted to open the innings, recovered much of his old form; while Wilf Slack and Keith Tomlins made marked advances. Much now is hoped of Andrew Miller, the Oxford left-hander. The supply of talent continues: and must be credited to Don Bennett, an outstanding coach.

Enjoy: the massive power of Wayne Daniel; the fielding of Graham Barlow.

NORTHAMPTONSHIRE

Northamptonshire continued one of the strongest batting, and weakest bowling, sides in the country. They had much ill-luck with their bowlers: Kapil Dev played in only seven matches; and the lately imported South African, James Carse, bought his 22 wickets expensively at 32.68 (ironically, with the aid of eight not-outs, he finished top of their batting averages). The departure of the obviously unhappy Peter Willey was a genuine loss. They could look to the future with increased confidence after the acquisition of Rupert ('Spook') Hanley, a hard-working, and consistently successful, Currie Cup seam-up bowler from Transvaal.

Tim Lamb, an honest self-critic, left and took up the post of Secretary of Middlesex. On the credit side, though, Neil Mallender, fast medium, shows marked improvement; and Jim Griffiths plugs gamely away. Crucially, though, in 1983 Northamptonshire were saved from virtual annihilation by the spin bowling of that faithful old master, David Steele (who then passed 20,000 runs, 500 wickets and 500 catches), and Richard Williams with his newly improved off-spin. Much is still needed; probably more than Hanley can provide.

Enjoy: the entertaining attacking batting of Wayne Larkins; the sheer – almost old-fashioned – professionalism of David Steele.

NOTTINGHAMSHIRE

After several seasons of advance, Nottinghsmshire passed into near eclipse and fourteenth position in 1983, largely through uneven batting. They had to expect to do better in that department with Clive Rice's recovery from injury, Derek Randall's release from the preoccupations of his benefit season, and the more frequent availability of Richard Hadlee.

They will, too, expect much from the acquisition of Chris Broad, a solid left-handed opening bat from Gloucestershire. Tim Robinson, too, seems to have both tightened and lifted his game, and he has an enterprising approach. Basharat Hassan is always doing something useful; and might well do more lower in the order. The bowling missed Eddie Hemmings's spin when he was injured. Above all, it was practically and psychologically weakened if it did not include Richard Hadlee, one of the finest all-rounders in the world when, as in 1983, he could appear only in five – as it happened, rain-interrupted – matches. The bowlers Peter Such and Andrew Pick, and the highly promising batsman, Paul Johnson – all capped for the England under-nineteen side – are fine prospects for the future. Granted fitness of key players – and the availability of Richard Hadlee is absolutely crucial – Nottinghamshire must challenge for all the honours for some years to come.

Enjoy: Derek Randall's immense delight in the game; Richard Hadlee's immense competitive urge; the Trent Bridge Hotel (historically the TBI).

SOMERSET

With their staff of highly talented players Somerset, who have never yet won the County Championship, have constantly challenged strongly for it in recent years; and have achieved success in the one-day competitions. In anticipation of losing the brilliant and entertaining Viv Richards to the West Indies' England tour of 1984, they signed the New Zealander Martin Crowe for a one-year contract; while their second West Indian, the monumentally accurate Joel Garner, was doubtful of choice for the tour on grounds of fitness.

They would expect to lose a fit Ian Botham to England's Test Matches; and perhaps Vic Marks as well. That must throw much batting responsibility on the shoulders of Peter Roebuck who remains one of the most interesting and promising players in the country. Their batting strength, apart from Peter Denning – valuable over-limit player and fine fieldsman – and Phil Slocombe, who simply has not redeemed his great promise, lies with the promising but largely unfledged Nigel Felton, Richard Ollis, and the all-rounder, Nigel Popplewell.

The bowling hinges on Joel Garner and Ian Botham, and struggles without them. Colin Dredge, though, gives game support in seam bowling; and still much is hoped of the faster Peter Wilson if only he can escape injury. The spin is generally in the hands of the off-spinners, Vic Marks and Jeremy Lloyds; but they may be challenged by the Yorkshire-born off-spinner, Booth. Happily for Somerset, Trevor Gard stepped most competently into the shoes of Derek Taylor.

Enjoy: the glorious batting of Viv Richards; the hitting and slip-catching of Ian Botham; buffet lunch at The Castle Hotel (two stars in Michelin: well worth the walk and missing the first half-hour of the afternoon).

SURREY

The retirement of Robin Jackman left the Surrey bowling, especially with the new ball, crucially weak. Until it is tightened they must expect to draw more matches than they win. Sylvester Clarke, one of the fastest bowlers in the world, tends to become uneconomically bouncer-happy; and David Thomas to lose his line. Both could become immensely more effective with more control. Graham Monkhouse shows the virtues of accuracy. Meanwhile the experienced 'Percy' Pocock remains one of the finest and most intelligent spin bowlers in the world.

The batting, of course, is strong. Geoffrey Howarth, who took over the captaincy from Roger Knight – still occasionally available as an all-rounder – plus the potentially brilliant Monte Lynch, the young Duncan Pauline, reliable Alan Butcher, solid Grahame Clinton and wicketkeeper, Jack Richards, ensure that David Smith will not be significantly missed; and Alec Stewart promises handsomely.

Enjoy: the bright batting of Monte Lynch; the high pace of Sylvester Clarke; the mellow skills of 'Percy' Pocock.

SUSSEX

Into the 1980s, Sussex depended so much on Imran Khan – one of the fastest bowlers and finest all-rounders in the world – that they seemed at a complete loss when he was absent or – despite his fine batting – unable to bowl. John Barclay, one of the most alert captains and formerly a successful one, seemed to lose confidence, and his batting and bowling fell off after he suffered persistent finger damage. An injury to Ian Greig increased his worries; and a third overseas player, Garth le Roux, lost much of his bowling edge. There is much talent available on the staff. The loss of confidence, though, seemed to extend to the promising Wells brothers, Colin and Alan, and even more to Paul Parker, lately regarded as a Test possible, who lost his team place in 1983. All this, of course, was psychological. In a heartened team the pace-bowling effort of Tony Pigott, the slow, left-arm skill of Chris Waller, the emerging ability, at fast-medium, of Dermot Reeve and the consistently skilful, and often brilliant, batting of Gehan Mendis, could combine to take Sussex back to their quality and success of 1981, when they were runners-up in the Championship.

Enjoy: the exciting batting of Gehan Mendis; the cover fielding of Paul Parker; the batting and bowling of Imran Khan; the wine bar and the Italian restaurant in Church Street, Hove; and the wine bar just outside the Saffrons at Eastbourne.

WARWICKSHIRE

The rise in Championship position from bottom to fifth that Warwickshire achieved in 1983 could be attributed largely to the bowling of their two experienced recruits, Norman Gifford from Worcestershire, and Chris Old from Yorkshire; respectively slow left-arm and right-arm medium. They, like Willis, can hardly prove so effective for much longer, but they can afford the naturally fast Gladstone Small the chance to develop, and Willie Hogg to regain his old form; and, meanwhile, the hard-working all-rounder, Anton Ferriera, provides sound ballast. The batting is extremely strong: the spectacular Alvin Kallicharran, the mature Dennis Amiss, the younger David Smith and Phil Oliver, and the thumping Geoff Humpage are capable of plenty of runs. Now they must watch the progress of Paul Smith, Asif Din, Simon Sutcliffe and Robin Dyer.

Enjoy: the opulent stroke-play of Alvin Kallicharran; the leg-spin of Asif Din – when he gets a game and a bowl.

WORCESTERSHIRE

Phil Neale seemed to be leading his young team along a fairly un-promising road until the county acquired David Smith and Kapil Dev. If Smith can realize his potential and – less likely – if Kapil Dev remains fit for a season, those two, plus occasionally, perhaps, the explosive West Indian, Collis King, could more than make good the loss of Younis.

Of the batsmen, Alan Ormrod, Phil Neale and Dipak Patel should continue long and valuably while the young Damian D'Oliveira, Martin Weston and Tim Curtis grow into the side. Pridgeon has sustained the pace bowling, while another West Indian, the eighteen-year-old Ricardo Ellcock, and Alan Warner are brought along. Altogether the prospect for Phil Neale looks far more encouraging than it did. Most, though, will probably depend on the spin-bowling pairing of Dipak Patel and the Yorkshire-born Richard Illingworth, which could become the county's most powerful attacking force.

Enjoy: the cover fielding of Phil Neale; the hitting of Collis King; the fast-bowling development of Ricardo Ellcock; the restaurant in the pavilion; the view of the cathedral.

YORKSHIRE

The current fortunes of the Yorkshire cricket team – or, for that matter, of the Yorkshire Cricket Club – bear little relationship to the playing ability of their cricketers. In 1983, this formerly eminent club fell to bottom position in the Championship, which made their John Player League win seem even more undignified. No other county has ever suffered such degradation; certainly not through the actions of people who, in the last analysis, did not give a damn for the welfare of the club, nor that of the game of cricket.

The newly appointed captain for 1984, David Bairstow, is a fine wicketkeeper, a bustling, enterprising batsman, and a cricketer of good heart. Richard Lumb, Neil Hartley, and even Ray Illingworth himself, seemed to have been affected by off-the-field influences. Most happily, Ashley Metcalfe and Martyn Moxon made impressive early marks, as batsmen; and so did Simon Dennis as a pace bowler. Jim Love batted both responsibly and consistently, while Kevin Sharp and Phil Carrick seemed to blossom late in the season – if that had any significance.

Steven Rhodes, Bairstow's understudy, and Paul Booth – slow left-arm – both appeared for Young England; but Alan Ramage, who had seemed such a fine pace-bowling prospect, was often unfit and unhappy. Geoff Boycott remains technically as fine a defensive batsman as any in the country, if not in the world.

It is not likely to be possible to pass fair judgement on the cricketers of Yorkshire, *qua* cricketers, until the club has undergone radical heart surgery.

Chapter 15

A SHORT BOOKLIST

Plenty of sound and helpful books exist for the cricket watcher who wants background reading. The chief problem is that many of the best are out of print. That has created a demand for specialist cricket book dealers. The best-known are E. K. Brown of Bevois Mount, Church Street, Liskeard, Cornwall; J. W. McKenzie, 12 Stoneleigh Park Road, Ewell, Surrey, KT19 0QT; and Martin Wood, 2 St John's Road, Sevenoaks, Kent, TN13 3LW. All three issue catalogues and keep a stock of antiquarian and out-of-print titles.

By far the best available reference book is *Barclay's World of Cricket*, edited by E. W. Swanton and John Woodcock, which has been lately brought up-to-date. There is a considerable and growing interest in the statistical side of the game: indeed there is an Association of Cricket Statisticians. (Secretary is P. Wynne-Thomas, Haughton Mill, Retford, Notts.)

It is sadly true that books of cricket statistics are out of date as soon as they are published – or before – but the two best basic volumes are those by Bill Frindall, *The Wisden Book of Test Cricket 1876–77 to 1977–78* and *The Wisden Book of Cricket Records*. The best exposition of the technique of the game is in *The MCC Cricket Coaching Book*; the work of several experts, it has been several times revised and is the authoritative work on the subject.

A booklet of *The Laws of Cricket* is published by MCC and there is also a manual of cricket umpiring and scoring, including the laws and interpretations and definitions for umpires, scorers, players and spectators by Tom Smith.

A History of Cricket by H. S. Altham and E. W. Swanton has been enlarged and extended since Harry Altham's one-volume work first appeared in 1926. It now runs to two volumes; a readable and scholarly survey.

The running account, as it might be called, of cricket history is the bulky *Wisden Cricketers' Almanack* (1299 pages in 1982), published annually since its first appearance in 1864. All the Test-playing countries, and some others, have annuals; and many have periodicals, of which the two best known in Britain are *The Cricketer International* (first published in 1921) and *Wisden Cricket Monthly*.

There are histories, statistics and studies of every aspect of the game; indeed, E. W. Padwick's *Bibliography of Cricket* contained 8294 titles when it was published in 1977; and well over a hundred fresh titles appear every year. Every enthusiast can follow his or her own particular interest. It may be worth mentioning, though, that those interested in the general appreciation – contemplation and enjoyment – of the game will find pleasure in the writings of Sir Neville Cardus, R. C. Robertson-Glasgow and Ray Robinson; while a diverting anthology, which also gives a view of the literature of the game, is *The Cricketer's Companion*, edited by Alan Ross.

There is a mounting interest in the collection of cricketana; and Phillips, the auctioneers, of Blenstock House, 7, Blenheim Street, New Bond Street, London WIY 0AS, hold periodic sales of cricket books and other collectors' items.